Ethical and Spiritual Values in Counseling

Edited by

Mary Thomas Burke, PhD
Judith G. Miranti, EdD

BF
637
.C6
E77
1992

Copyright © 1992 by the Association for Religious and
Value Issues in Counseling (ARVIC)

All rights reserved.

American Association for Counseling and Development
5999 Stevenson Avenue
Alexandria, VA 22304

Cover Design by Sarah Jane Valdez

Library of Congress Cataloging-in-Publication Data

Ethical and spiritual values in counseling / edited by Mary Thomas Burke,
  Judith G. Miranti.
    p. cm.
  Includes bibliographical references.
  ISBN 1-556520-094-3
  1. Counseling—Moral and ethical aspects. 2. Psychotherapy—Moral and ethical
aspects. 3. Spirituality. I. Burke, Mary Thomas. II. Miranti, Judith G.
BF637.C6E77 1992
174'915—dc20
                                                                91-46799
                                                                     CIP

Printed in the United States of America

Dedication

*The editors dedicate this volume to our parents
and the ARVIC pioneers who gave us a legacy
that we are privileged to share*

and

*to our families for their support
and encouragement always.*

Table of Contents

Foreword — vii
Preface — ix

Ethics and Spirituality: The Prevailing Forces Influencing the Counseling Profession — 1
  Judith Miranti and Mary Thomas Burke

Three Contributions of a Spiritual Perspective to Counseling, Psychotherapy, and Behavior Change — 5
  Allen E. Bergin

Utilization of Spiritual Values in Counseling: An Ignored Dimension — 17
  Robert M. Theodore

The Counselor and Religious Dilemma: A Personal Experience — 23
  C. Edward Watkins, Jr.

The Moral Nature of Psychotherapy — 27
  Barry Grant

The Morality of Influencing in Counseling — 37
  John M. Schulte

Guilt — 53
  David Belgum

Psychotherapy as a Process of Value Stabilization — 67
  Jeff Schwehn and Candace Garrett Schau

Values and Ethics in Family Therapy — 75
  William J. Doherty

Therapist and Family Values in a Cultural Context — 81
  Howard F. Stein

The Values of Counseling: Three Domains — 93
  Edwin L. Herr and Spencer Niles

Table of Contents

Values in Counseling and Psychotherapy   107
    C. H. Patterson

Counseling the Culturally Different   121
    C. Jerry Downing

Ethical Issues in Gerocounseling   127
    Marion L. Cavallaro and Marylou Ramsey

Object Relations and the Development of Values   135
    George M. Gazda and Charlalee Sedgwick

The Impact of Contemporary Idealogy and AIDS on the Counseling of Gay Clients   143
    James Rudolph

ARVIC as a Child of Ten   155
    Samuel T. Gladding

Foreword

I am very enthusiastic about *Ethical and Spiritual Values in Counseling*, compiled by Mary Thomas Burke and Judith Miranti. This volume is a selection of some excellent articles which were published in *Counseling and Values*.

As editor of *Counseling and Values* from 1984–1990, I was directly involved in the evaluation of the majority of the articles in this volume. Mary Thomas Burke and Judith Miranti are to be commended for their selections. The articles address a number of specific issues and populations including family therapy, individual counseling and psychotherapy, career counseling, and philosophical issues regarding values and ethics. The selection of articles also provides a balance of informative and stimulating "thought pieces" with research studies.

The process of counseling is strongly a moralistic and values enterprise, as well as a scientific enterprise. Ethics and spirituality are inexorably interwoven into the systematic process of helping clients change. Mary Thomas Burke and Judith Miranti have done an excellent service for the members of AACD and ARVIC who are interested in the roles ethics, spirituality, and values play in the counseling process. I believe this volume will serve as a useful resource for counselors and counselor educators. Also, the readings will stimulate thought and discussion and that is always the mark of a useful book.

Nicholas Colangelo
Professor, Counselor Education
The University of Iowa

Preface

In this age of electronic mail, media blitz and instantaneous universal information explosion, professional counselors are fortunate to have professional ethical guidelines which act as their "magna carta." Since each case needs to be examined for its own merit and new insights have evolved as professional counselors have struggled with new issues such as AIDS, the ethical dimensions of counseling must become of paramount importance to all practitioners.

Concurrent with the ethical values, the editors believe that spirituality is at the core of one's search for meaning. If a person's primary need is for this meaning and if meaning gives purpose to behavior, an individual's search for meaning is a life-sustaining endeavor. The choices and resulting behaviors emanating from a value system are not separate, independent, or isolated occurrences, but rather are integrally bound to that system. The very core of our existence depends on one's ability to remain centered and focused while struggling to exercise the freedom to grow and transcend life's difficult choices.

There may be a few who will dare to investigate the possibility that there is a lawful reality which is not open to our five senses, a reality in which present, past, and future are intermingled (Rogers, 1973). Rogers's statement underlies the basic tenet which the authors' believe. That is, if we can accept concepts such as self-worth, self-esteem, and self-actualization, if counseling finds these topics worthy of exploration, then it is just as legitimate to explore the concept of spirituality.

Not to include spirituality is to refuse to look at significant influences on human behavior and one's inherent ability to go beyond the ordinary everyday experiences. Choice lies in options and decisions regarding what is ethical and their choices are the result of an intergenerational value system. The authors in this volume have attempted to bring into sharper focus the ethical and spiritual dimension in counseling, in the hope that once the present-centered concept of spirituality is developed, the journey into the future-oriented world of hope can begin.

In particular we want to thank the Board of Directors of ARVIC, without whose support this project would not have been possible. For their reading of the manuscript and their helpful feedback, we are especially grateful to Dom Pellegreno, Richard Mucowski, Ann Marie Wallace, and Phyllis Post.

We sincerely hope that this volume will be helpful to our professional colleagues as we journey together with our clients in search of meaning in our lives.

Mary Thomas Burke
Judith G. Miranti

Ethics and Spirituality: The Prevailing Forces Influencing the Counseling Profession

**JUDITH MIRANTI
MARY THOMAS BURKE**

AS COUNSELORS PROGRESS through the last decade of the twentieth century, they need to address the spiritual and ethical issues that confront them. This book is an effort to respond to this need. The editors of this volume have reviewed the issues of the *Counseling and Values Journal* published during the last decade and selected those articles in the journals that seemed most relevant to the topics of ethics and spirituality in counseling and psychotherapy. The authors of these articles are among the leaders in the counseling profession and bring together some current thinking on these very critical issues.

In this introductory essay, an attempt will be made to present an overview of the prevailing forces influencing the counseling profession and to address topics the authors of the articles have critically examined. This work will be a resource for professionals who seek to help their clients contemplate spiritual and ethical issues which have meaning for their lives.

The search for meaning and spiritual integration is as dynamic and ongoing as the search for truth. This search is a journey of transition from self-centeredness to self-transcendence, from the false self to the true self, from isolation and alienation to a mature relationship involving intimacy, altruism, and love. As each phase or transition is experienced, values are placed on those things that can help persons achieve happiness and success. Infants and young persons are quick to perceive how they can get needs met and act accordingly. In the young adult phase, actions are motivated by personal gain and acceptance. In the adult phase, actions are governed by professional competence and recognition. In the middle years, introspective processes are begun at what might be called a stopping point for reassessment of one's life as well as assessing one's undeveloped inner resources. Thus, life's passage can be renegotiated and made more meaningful.

These transitions are both deeply psychological and spiritual. The one at mid-life may involve the renegotiation of one's dreams and also of one's self ideal self born of youth. Negative or shadow dimensions often become apparent along with the stark awareness of mortality. When this occurs the foothold on life appears to be lost and the experience is painful. The darkness experienced is both sad and joyful, because from the renegotiation there comes a deeper and richer life. What emerges is the authentic self open to the infinite. Ideals are replaced with an anxious sense of reality. Thus, resolve is fortified and strengthened, and meaning appears before it is too late to reap the fruits of the laboring years.

At times, however, the spiritual need seems more important. Hopefully, an examination of those times of transition and need will become insightful as to what of importance has occurred or is occurring. When the most vulnerability is felt, the need for spiritual nourishment becomes more necessary. Is vulnerability essential for intimacy? Does exposing the true self enable the closest communication possible between individuals? Does this allow the essence of the true self to become one with another person? Is this what gives meaning to life? All of these questions must be considered by those in the counseling profession whose major obligation it is to promote good mental health.

Good mental health can be defined as the balance and integration of all the dimensions of personhood. There occurs a longing for, and a desiring of, the transcendent and a connection with the mysterious "other." Does this mean that the spiritual dimension is integral to wholeness and personal integrity? If yes, then why the resistance and conflict as to whether or not it is proper to explore this dimension in the counseling setting? Would it violate the ethical code if spiritual issues were addressed? Is counseling concerned only with intellectual, social, psychological, and physical aspects of wholeness? Perhaps what can be learned from the model used in chemical dependency is that recovery is not effected without the commitment of the spiritual component which is essential for healing. Are psychotherapists and counseling professionals at a crossroads where it is no longer necessary to apologize for, or to defend, the roles played by spirituality and religion in therapy?

The 1960s were referred to as the era of value-free counseling. In the 1970s counseling began to be seriously accepted as a profession with its own credentialing authorities. In the 1980s, a pioneering movement was begun to incorporate the hitherto ignored dimensions of spirituality and religious beliefs into the therapeutic process and to recognize transpersonal psychology, the Fourth Force in Psychology. Can more time be wasted in arguing for or against the need to address these dimensions? Because emphasis is placed on wellness and the acceptance of this as a developmental model for mental well-being, all components of wellness, including the spiritual dimension, must be addressed if balance and personal integration is to occur.

In an effort to respond to some of these basic questions the editors have included in this volume a sampling of articles addressing ethical and spiritual concerns of counselors. The following is a brief overview of the articles which have been included.

A movement gaining acceptance is a widespread cultural phenomenon—that of returning to the study of values, including spiritual ones. Bergin (1986) outlined his template which can be divided into three areas in which a spiritual perspective is a positive contribution to psychological thought and practice. Encouraging counselors to be sensitive to the client's religious background and accompanying personal values was the intent of Theodore (1984) as he facilitated the exploration of spiritual attitudes and feelings in the relief of psychic suffering. Watkins (1982) shared his personal experiences as he attempted to put aside his religious biases to promote clients' understanding of their own religious dilemmas.

Today, most counselors/psychotherapists no longer believe that psychotherapy is a value-free process. Beneath talk of research, theory, techniques, modalities, legal concerns, and professional images are positions of values and morals. Grant (1985) cautioned us to be careful about personal attitudes of counselors/therapists and their perceptions of the dynamic function of morality and guilt. What the counselor or therapist believed, wrote Belgum (1985), about the function of morality and guilt was also of significance and deemed to affect both diagnosis and treatment.

Doherty (1985) contended that ethical concerns and human values were continually re-evaluated by each new generation. An inquiry into the place of values in therapy is a tool that can enable therapists to understand the ways in which they seek to intervene. Herr and Niles (1988) insisted that rather than consider the possibility that the counselor's values and the intervention strategy used may run counter to the client's values system, the danger lies in the counselor labeling the client. It is unfortunate that the counselor does not understand the client's value system or its possible cultural antecedent, wrote Herr and Niles (1988). When this occurs, premature termination of the therapeutic relationship could result. Hence, they supported the need for counselors to be aware of not only how their values affected the process, but how the knowledge of the clients' value systems was essential for the continuation of the relationship.

According to Patterson (1989), it was important to realize that therapists were first persons and second, clinicians who were participating in relationships with clients. He suggested an approach to counseling and psychotherapy values that were basic to the development of persons in the process of self-actualization and also incorporated them in his work. Stein (1985), on the other hand, was concerned about whether or not counselors had access to information relative to the issues.

Downing (1982) exhorted counselors to learn about the individual culture of their clients and the impact of their own culture and of their biases toward others. He further contended that clients were the best source of data about their own cultures. He challenged his students in training to address and deal with their cultural biases.

Counselors have been, and are, constantly faced with ethical dilemmas. These have become more complicated as emerging populations with a new generation of problems, such as AIDS, come to the fore. The growing population of the elderly also has differing needs. Much research needs to be done in these areas, because as persons face their imminent mortality, many are more anxious to explore their own spiritual values to find the meaning of life. Some work has been done in this area. Cavallero and Ramsey (1988) examined the unique ethical issues in gerontological counseling. They forecast that as this field grows, new issues pertaining to the practice of counseling with the elderly will arise. In their article, various dilemmas are enumerated and ways to address them are considered.

For counselors, the challenge for the 1990s is not whether the issues of spirituality, values, and ethics should be addressed, but how they can best be handled. Societal forces should become mandates that these dilemmas be seriously examined.

Three Contributions of a Spiritual Perspective to Counseling, Psychotherapy, and Behavior Change

ALLEN E. BERGIN

TRADITIONAL THERAPEUTIC MOVEMENTS, such as the behavioral and psychoanalytic approaches, were established upon a mechanistic and naturalistic conceptual foundation that deliberately excluded spiritual perspectives. This was done for good historical reasons (Boring, 1950) and it provided a structure and stimulus for advances in the field that probably would not otherwise have occurred (Freud, 1917; Skinner, 1953; Wolpe, 1958). Despite some advantages, the premises of these orientations failed to provide a comprehensive account of human functioning; consequently, alternative positions have gradually developed that are now opening the theoretical domain to radically different concepts.

The humanistic movement, for example, has emphasized a different view of human nature and of the change process. Although it continued to omit the spiritual in its earlier versions, it opened a new vision of human potentialities that liberated human behavior studies from their mechanical strictures (Maslow, 1954; Rogers, 1961). The counseling and development field, with its concern for student growth and for health as opposed to pathology, was already oriented in this direction; consequently, it derived strength from the humanistic movement and in turn strongly reinforced the basic trends in humanistic theories. Both of these influential streams in therapeutic thought have also provided support for the new spiritual perspectives that are developing, as is evidenced by the later views of Maslow (1971) and Rogers (1980), and by a steady flow of publications in the journal of *Counseling and Values*.

Recently, the cognitive movement has added strength to the shift away from mechanism and naturalism by combining an agentive perspective with rigorous research (Bandura, 1986; Mischel, 1986). Social, cognitive, and affective variables have become important explanatory tools, and theorists are dealing with a level of complexity and internal nuance that is far beyond the hydraulic mechanisms of psychodynamics and the elementary notions of control via stimulus-response connections.

All of these trends have stretched our conceptual foundations, and there has, therefore, arisen a paradigmatic crisis. Professional values are being shaken in the process, and the shifting theoretical structure has opened the naturalistic philosophical monolith to spiritual factors that go beyond all previous concepts in personality theory, including the recently emphasized cognitive-agentive theories (Bergin, 1980a, 1983; Collins, 1977; Spilka, Hood, & Gorsuch, 1985).

This does not mean to me entirely abandoning the former structure, but instead, building upon it by adding another cornerstone. There may well be specific "mechanisms" in personality and change processes, but they do not ordinarily constitute the dominating force that was once thought. Freud and Skinner clearly saw certain aspects of behavioral nature, but they erred in overgeneralizing from limited observations. It is timely to add a spiritual keystone to the building blocks already provided by the behavioral, psychodynamic, humanistic, life-span developmental, and cognitive approaches.

A cogent argument needs to be given for launching in this direction rather than mindlessly reverting to medieval notions of what the "spiritual" entails. There is, therefore, a growing substantive literature, which is interdisciplinary in nature, that addresses these matters (cf. Bergin, 1980a, 1985). A full narration of arguments and evidences is beyond the scope of this article, but three implications for psychotherapy and behavior therapy that are of immediate importance are described below.

In this context, it is important to recognize that a movement is occurring. It is a widespread cultural phenomenon, a return to the study of values, including spiritual values, but it is happening with new sophistication and more systematic and empirical analysis (Bergin, 1986). This trend is happening in various parts of the world (Gomez & Currea, 1983) and is not confined only to Judeo-Christian nations or traditions. Many new organizations and new journals have been formed. This movement did not begin at one point in time but it began to gather momentum in the early 1970s and may eventually reach the point of becoming an orientation (Bergin, 1980a).

In what follows, I put my own template on what is happening and describe it from the personal perspective of one participant. My template can be divided into three areas that a spiritual perspective contributes to psychological thought and practice. The first is a conception of human nature, the second is a moral frame of reference, and the third is a set of techniques. The description of these contributions will be necessarily selective for the purposes of this brief account.

A CONCEPTION OF HUMAN NATURE

With regard to theory, the most important notion is that there is a spiritual reality and that spiritual experiences make a difference in our behavior. This thesis is an essential centerpiece in a spiritual orientation, but it must be subjected to tests in the same manner that invisible realities in biology and physics are subjected to tests.

For instance, are verbal reports of religious experience correlated with important criterion variables, such as mental health? This question has been studied more thoroughly than most therapists are aware of (cf. Bergin, 1983, for a review), and new studies are underway. We have been exploring the question of healthy and unhealthy religious experiences using a test battery and interview ratings. There is definitely a kind of religious experience that professional observers see as having healthy consequences as measured by usual observational methods (Bergin, Masters, & Richards, 1987; Bergin, Stinchfield, Gaskin, Masters, & Sullivan, 1988). These experiences are similar to Allport's concept of intrinsic religiousness (Allport & Ross, 1967).

It is not necessary to be committed to a theory of spiritual realities to conduct such studies, nor are the results of the studies conclusive evidence of such phenomena. The self-reports do, however, provide a basis for making inferences about possibly powerful aspects of human nature that are unlikely to be inferred by means of other theories. Whether these inferences are more scientifically fertile than others remains to be evaluated through rigorous inquiry. Marks (1978) referred to this possibility after examining instances of dramatic behavior change consequent on religious experiences:

> When it works, faith healing has a power for surpassing existing psychotherapy technology. The order of magnitude of this difference is like that between nuclear and more conventional explosives. But we have not yet harnessed nuclear power satisfactorily, and our understanding of faith and religious processes is far more primitive than our knowledge of subatomic particles. Given a prepared mind, however, some paths into this labyrinth might be laid down. The important point is for hard-nosed experimenters to be alive to these possibilities, while retaining their methodological rigor. (p. 530)

Inferring the specific structures and process involved in such phenomena is yet to be done, but the procedure is not different in principle from inferences made about invisible and indescribable "genes" in the history of biology, or subatomic particles in the history of physics. Such concepts were enormously useful for a long time as indirect evidence before electron microscopes and other procedures made direct observation feasible. These scientific developments may have more similarity to the quest for the spiritual than the historical estrangement between science and religion suggests. Although spiritual phenomena may not be directly analogous to these other aspects of nature, rigorous study may make them far more amenable to systematic treatment than is now the case.

Some of our colleagues are obviously enthused about these possibilities, as is evidenced by the items in the reference list. Others are distressed by the prospect that such work could result in a regression to magical, or at least unscientific, thinking, a reversion to reliance on dogma or other dilutions of hard-won scientific progress (Ellis, 1980).

It is not necessary, however, to approach the spiritual in terms of traditional notions of the "supernatural." What is spiritual may be different from ordinary matter, but it still seems to be natural in that it proceeds according to laws or principles. Assuming that there is such a thing as a spiritual substance, it may be possible eventually to harmonize the principles governing it with empirical, behavioral, and materialist positions.

Our own studies of people who report spiritual experiences seem to manifest connections between those experiences and the material world, such as in those behaviors that reflect mental status and life style. We have noted, for instance, several cases in which conversion experiences provided powerful compensating effects for pathologies in individuals' lives (Bergin et al., 1988). We are also interested in the effects of such experiences on physical health and whether there is anything beyond their relaxing effects, such as those noted in transcendental meditation. There is also some evidence from Antonovsky's work (1979) that the sense of coherence in life that is derived from spiritual convictions is correlated with physical health.

It is, of course, difficult to embrace within the same frame of reference both mechanistic notions, such as the existence of classically conditioned responses and the idea that people have a mental apparatus with cognitive, agentive, and spiritual aspects. This is made much easier by assuming that the psychobehavioral aspects of organisms are multisystemic, just as the biological aspects are. Our bodies consist of semi-independent circulatory, nervous, muscular, skeletal, and other systems. These depend upon each other, yet they also are entities unto themselves that follow very different laws, for example, the hydraulic laws of the circulatory system and the electrochemical laws of the nervous system. The laws of one system are not necessarily applicable to another system. If this is true for the body, it may also be true for one's psychology.

It is conceivable, then, that there is a system that functions according to classical conditioning which coexists alongside other systems having to do with agentive processes and spiritual processes, each having a part to play in the organic whole. Such "systems" are yet to be identified, differentiated, and described, but their possible existence makes it potentially feasible to harmonize seemingly incompatible perspectives on how human beings function.

To me, the spiritual area is a rich source of hypotheses and intriguing problems for inquiry. Although it remains to be seen whether a uniquely "spiritual" theoretical structure is needed to explain the phenomena being described in modern studies, whatever the outcome is, it should help us understand better the spiritual experiences that most human beings report (Gallup Organization, 1985) and whether they are related to psychologically important behaviors.

A MORAL FRAME OF REFERENCE

The second important contribution of a spiritual perspective is that it anchors values in universal terms. This is important because therapeutic interventions are not value-free. Values determine the goals of treatment, the selection of techniques, and the evaluation of outcomes (London, 1986; Lowe, 1976).

Three Contributions of a Spiritual Perspective

What values determine the goals of treatment? How do we set those goals? All goals, whether they are goals for symptom relief or goals to modify a lifestyle, are subtended by value systems. Elsewhere, I have argued that we generally seek to base our professional value decisions upon basic principles, and I cited Strupp's statement that major value themes seem to be universal (Bergin, 1985). This notion has been echoed by other people. Maslow, for example, was among the strongest advocates of such a view when he said, "Instead of cultural relativity, I'm implying that there are basic underlying human standards that are cross-cultural. Psychologists who advocate moral and cultural relativism are not coming to grips with the real problem" (Goble, 1971, p. 92).

Ethical relativism is not consistent with the idea that there are laws of human behavior, nor is it consistent with the specifically targeted goals of behavior modification (Kitchener, 1980). It is true that there is *cultural* relativism, that is, cultures differ and individuals differ in their values. But this does not mean that *ethical* relativism is true, that is, the notion that different ethics are equally valid or that different cultures are equally viable. Human growth, then, may be regulated in part by moral principles comparable in exactness with physical or biological laws, a position adeptly argued by Campbell (1976) in his APA presidential address.

Some writers, however, object to this thesis on the grounds that it has absolutistic tendencies. They say it is tainted by authoritarian, narrow, and judgmental frames of reference that are incompatible with the personal freedom that we prize and that we attempt to promote in our therapeutic interventions (Ellis, 1980). However, arguments that pit universals or absolutes against freedom oversimplify the situation. Obedience to moral values is in principle no different from obedience to physical laws. We are free to launch a space shuttle into orbit only if we precisely obey the natural principles that make it possible. It may be that behavioral laws are just as precise, and obedience to them just as essential for obtaining desirable and predictable consequences. The freedom to self-actualize, for instance, is predicated on obedience to the laws by which self-actualization is possible. Thus, the thinking that sets conformity to moral law (i.e., values) against individual freedom and then repudiates ethical universals is inconsistent and misleading (Bergin, 1980b).

If we take seriously the existence of universals, as a large proportion of clinical thinkers do (Bergin, 1985), then the importance of guiding constructs for orienting choices and goals of clients becomes more evident. It seems that the laws pertinent to mental health should influence the way we construe disorders, how we activate clients' agentive capacities, and the responsibilities we expect them to take for their actions. We observe regularly such patterns of cognitive evaluation and choosing in our clients as we discern the causes of their pain and suffering, as well as the changes that bring release and hope. Our awareness that certain principles underlie the processes of disturbance and therapeutic improvement anchors the way we think about therapy and the way we influence clients' views about how they might regulate their lives. This then provides them with cognitive structures (including values) for organizing the behavior being suggested by the therapist.

A good example of the application of the concept of universals is in the therapeutic attempt to promote self-control, a common practice in modern therapy. Enhancing self-control of impulses, addictions, or other nonadaptive habits is critical. Such self-regulation is enhanced by a belief that the regulation is valuable, and that it leads to long-term consequences beneficial to the client and to those who are important to the client. In this respect, the therapist is in the role of a teacher or an instructor who is trying to help the client reconstrue the world and incorporate in the construct system values concerning intrapsychic and interpersonal consequences of behavior.

Endorsing such values and making them explicit helps both the therapist and client realize that self-control can be guided in terms of possible universal themes. Self-regulation can never be optimally successful unless a commitment is made to values, and that commitment can be stronger and more lasting if the client feels that he or she is committing to something that is lawful and moral; not just because somebody said so but because it is built into the universe and is part of our nature.

Although there is some disagreement about which values are relevant to mental health, there is a surprising degree of consensus concerning a number of values that are generally used to guide therapeutic efforts. My own informal survey of professional therapists identified 23 value statements about which there seemed to be considerable agreement (Bergin, 1985), and a subsequent national survey (Jensen & Bergin, 1988) confirmed and extended these preliminary findings.

Jensen developed a survey based on value-laden statements in the professional literature and administered it to a national sample of mental health professionals in clinical psychology, marriage and family therapy, psychiatry, and clinical social work. Responses were elicited from 67% of the psychologists, 64% of the social workers, 63% of the marriage and family therapists, and 40% of the psychiatrists. The values that mental health professionals endorse concern (a) autonomy and responsibility, (b) perception and expression of feelings, (c) coping strategies, (d) physical health and fitness, (e) work satisfaction, (f) self-awareness and growth, (g) interpersonal skills and commitments, (h) marriage, family, and community involvement, (i) having a mature value system, and (j) responsible and fulfilling sexuality.

Some representative survey items that were considered mentally healthy and the percent out of 425 respondents agreeing to each item are as follows (high, medium, and low agreement inclusive): "Assume responsibility for one's actions" (100%); "Develop effective strategies for coping with stress" (100%); "Develop the ability to give and receive affection" (100%); "Increase

Three Contributions of a Spiritual Perspective

one's ability to be sensitive to others' feelings" (99%); "Increase one's capacity for self-control" (99%); "Have a sense of purpose for living" (97%); "Be open, genuine, and honest" (96%); "Find fulfillment or satisfaction in work" (97%); "Apply self-discipline in the use of alcohol, tobacco, and drugs" (95%); "Acquire an awareness of inner potential and capacity to grow" (96%); "Be faithful to one's marriage partner" (91%); "Be committed to family needs and child-rearing" (90%); "Increase one's respect for human value and worth" (89%); "Be able to forgive parents or others who have inflicted disturbance in oneself" (93%); "Be able to forgive oneself for mistakes that have hurt others" (97%); "Understand that sexual impulses are a natural part of oneself" (100%); and "Regard sexual relations as satisfying only when there is mutual consent of both partners" (94%).

There were many other specific items on which there was a surprising degree of agreement. There were also items on which the respondents were divided. For example: "Have preference for a heterosexual sex relationship" (57% agree, 7% uncertain, 36% disagree); "Become self-sacrificing and unselfish" (52% agree, 9% uncertain, 39% disagree); and "Have a religious affiliation in which one actively participates" (44% agree, 12% uncertain, 44% disagree). There was more division concerning specific spirituality/religiosity items than any other subgroup, but more general items pertaining to this topic elicited greater consensus, for example: "Seek a spiritual understanding of the universe and one's place in it" (68% agree, 9% uncertain, 23% disagree).

Although a survey does not, by itself, prove that therapists have well-developed therapeutic value systems, it does indicate that they believe certain values to be relevant and helpful to mental health and treatment strategies. As far as spiritual values are concerned, there is a definite difference of opinion, as we found in a previous debate (Bergin, 1980a, 1980b; Ellis, 1980; Walls, 1980). Among the survey respondents and in the field generally, there are differences on specific moral issues, but there is also considerable consensus on values that seem to be derived in a general way from the Judeo-Christian roots of our culture. To the extent that universals or "laws" are built into these values, as Strupp and Maslow suggested, they may form some elements of a therapeutic value system.

The importance of establishing a moral frame of reference is obvious to anyone who has carefully examined the value-laden nature of counselor interventions (London, 1986; Strupp & Hadley, 1977). To launch into modifying human behavior without a value perspective, as though such intervention is merely a technology applied to objectively defined disorders, fosters confusion. A spiritual orientation reemphasizes the importance of being open, specific, and deliberate about values. It helps us shed inhibitions about helping people activate values that can be used as cognitive guides in their self-regulation and lifestyles. In addition, it extends our values perspective beyond the narrow and immediate definition of good outcome that we are accustomed to by emphasizing the broad, social, and long-term aspects that make life meaningful and lifestyles fruitful, even across one's lifespan and into succeeding generations.

TECHNIQUES

The third contribution of a spiritual perspective constitutes a set of techniques (e.g., Collins, 1980). These range from intrapsychic methods, such as the use of prayer, scripture study, rituals, and inspirational counseling, to family and social system methods that use group support, communication, mutual participation, communal spiritual experience, and group identification. We have already noted Marks's reference to faith healing. In addition, it is possible to use traditional spiritual involvements within standard therapy (Lovinger, 1984; Spero, 1985; Stern, 1985).

I will describe here just one illustration of a technique. I refer to it as the "transitional figure" technique, in which the client is taught to become a transitional person in the history of his or her family by first assessing one's emotional genealogy. That is, the person is encouraged to see himself or herself as at a crossroads in his or her family history. As Erikson put it, the case history is embedded in history—the history at least of one's family as it precedes and succeeds the individual.

The transitional figure, the client, is taught that although he or she has been the victim of pathologizing events in life, and that although these events or persons caused a variety of pains and difficulties, it is important to adopt a forgiving attitude. That is, the release of aggression against the victimizing agents, although it may be important at certain therapeutic junctures, is not healing in a deep and lasting way.

We introduce, in this context, the concepts of sacrifice and redemption that are common to great religions, especially the Judeo-Christian tradition. In this we are not referring to the extremes to which that concept has been taken, but to the notion that the pain one is experiencing may have to be suffered in a certain way, that sometimes it is important to absorb the pain that has been handed down across generations. If your mother or father did it to you, do you necessarily blame them? Are there predecessors to their behaviors and to the behavior of those predecessors?

Is it important, then, for somebody, sometime in the history of a pathological family, to stop the process of transmitting pain from generation to generation? Instead of seeking retribution, one learns to absorb the pain, to be forgiving, to try to reconcile with forebears, and then become a generator of positive change in the next generation. The therapeutically changed individual thereby becomes intergenerationally transitional by resisting the disordered patterns of the past, exercising an interpersonally healing impact, and then transmitting to the younger generation a healthier mode of functioning. This pattern of conduct applies the ideal of the redeemer role in a therapeutically powerful way.

Some unusual changes have occurred in people who have adopted a role like this. One young woman had a bitter relationship with her father and expressed all of her negative feelings about him during therapy. The connections between his behavior and her problems seemed clear. After learning about the transitional figure idea, she was encouraged to go back to visit her father and, instead of confronting him with the pain he had caused, to invite him to tell her about his history and to do a family history interview. She was not to ask him about his dynamics or disturbances and their consequences, but instead, about his identity, experiences, and so forth.

The result of doing this, including tape-recording and transcribing the interviews with her father, caused a dramatic reconciliation between the woman and her father and a merging of perceptions of painful events that had occurred. It stimulated her father to face certain realities he had never faced. This was, however, a gentle experience occurring in a forgiving atmosphere. As a result, he was able to lower his defenses, apologize, and seek to make up for his past conduct. The changes in both client and father as a result of this encounter seemed to be dramatic and more profound than the changes that had been occurring through regular treatment (V.L. Brown, personal communication, October, 1977).

As in religious tradition, sacrifice was required on the part of the client, that is, she gave up the need for retribution and separation from the past family network. Furthermore, the sacrificial act, consisting of self-denial and forgiveness, yielded ultimate benefits to all parties that more than compensated for the sacrifice. The values that guided this process have been part of major human traditions for centuries. A spiritual perspective reminds us that the development and endurance of such traditions is not likely to have been accidental or irrelevant to the needs of human beings (Campbell, 1976).

In conclusion, the spiritual template we have placed over the therapeutic enterprise shows the possibilities in that perspective for an alternative theory of human nature, for clarifying how values can facilitate change, and for the development of new techniques. This review provides but the simplest introduction to an important and growing literature. It represents an orientation that marks a decided turn in the interests and sympathies of behavioral scientists (Bergin, 1986), but it is one that can be harmonized with and is supportive of our vital and unchanging commitment to empirical science and to human welfare.

REFERENCES

Allport, G. W., & Ross, J. M. (1967). Personal religious orientation and prejudice. *Journal of Personality and Social Psychology, 5,* 432–443.

Antonovsky, A. (1979). *Health, stress, and coping.* San Francisco: Jossey-Bass.

Bandura, A. (1986). *Social foundations of thought and action: A social-cognitive theory.* Englewood Cliffs, NJ: Prentice-Hall.

Bergin, A. E. (1980a). Psychotherapy and religious values. *Journal of Consulting and Clinical Psychology, 48,* 95–105.

Bergin, A. E. (1980b). Religious and humanistic values: A reply to Ellis and Walls. *Journal of Consulting and Clinical Psychology, 48,* 642–645.

Bergin, A. E. (1983). Religiosity and mental health: A critical reevaluation and meta-analysis. *Professional Psychology, 14,* 170–184.

Bergin, A. E. (1985). Proposed values for guiding and evaluating counseling and psychotherapy. *Counseling and Values, 29,* 99–116.

Bergin, A. E. (1986). Psychotherapy and religious factors. [A review of R. J. Lovinger's "Working with religious issues in therapy" and M. H. Spero's "Psychotherapy of the religious patient."] *Contemporary Psychology, 31,* 85–87.

Bergin, A. E., Masters, K. S., & Richards, P. S. (1987). Religiousness and mental health reconsidered: A study of an intrinsically religious sample. *Journal of Counseling Psychology, 34,* 197–204.

Bergin, A. E., Stinchfield, R., Gaskin, T., Masters, K. S., & Sullivan, C. (1988). Religious lifestyles and mental health: An exploratory study. *Journal of Counseling Psychology, 35,* 91–98.

Boring, E. G. (1950). *A history of experimental psychology* (2nd ed.). New York: Appleton-Century Crofts.

Campbell, D. T. (1976). On the conflicts between biological and social evolution and between psychology and moral tradition. *American Psychologist, 30,* 1103–1120.

Collins, G. R. (1977). *The rebuilding of psychology: An integration of psychology and Christianity.* Wheaton, IL: Tyndale.

Collins, G. R. (1980). *Christian counseling.* Waco, TX: Word Press.

Ellis, A. (1980). Psychotherapy and atheistic values: A response to A. E. Bergin's "Psychotherapy and religious values." *Journal of Consulting and Clinical Psychology, 48,* 635–639.

Freud, S. (1917). *A general introduction to psychoanalysis.* New York: Pocket Books (Simon & Schuster, 1973).

Gallup Organization. (1985). *Religion in America.* Princeton, NJ: Author.

Goble, F. G. (1971). *The third force: The psychology of Abraham Maslow.* New York: Pocket Books.

Gomez, A. P., & Currea, F. B. (1983). *Psicoterapias 1983: Perspectivas de integration.* Bogota, Columbia: Universidad de los Andes.

Jensen, J. P., & Bergin, A. E. (1988). Mental health values of professional therapists: A national interdisciplinary survey. *Professional Psychology: Research and Practice, 19,* 290–297.

Kitchener, R. F. (1980). Ethical relativism and behavior therapy. *Journal of Consulting and Clinical Psychology, 48,* 1–7.

London, P. (1986). *The modes and morals of psychotherapy* (2nd ed.). New York: Norton.

Lovinger, R. J. (1984). *Working with religious issues in therapy.* New York: Jason Aronson.

Lowe, C. M. (1976). *Value orientations in counseling and psychotherapy* (2nd ed.). Cranston, RI: Carroll Press.

Marks, I. M. (1978). Behavioral psychotherapy of adult neurosis. In S. L. Garfield and A. E. Bergin (Eds.), *Handbook of psychotherapy and behavior change* (pp. 493–547). New York: Wiley.

Maslow, A. H. (1954). *Motivation and personality.* New York: Harper.

Maslow, A. H. (1971). *The farther reaches of human nature.* New York: Viking.

Mischel, W. (1986). *Introduction to personality* (4th ed.). New York: Holt, Rinehart & Winston.

Rogers, C. R. (1961). *On becoming a person.* Boston: Houghton Mifflin.

Rogers, C. R. (1980). *A way of being.* Boston: Houghton Mifflin.

Skinner, B. F. (1953). *Science and human behavior.* New York: Free Press.

Spero, M. H. (Ed.). (1985). *Psychotherapy of the religious patient.* Springfield, IL: Charles C Thomas.

Spilka, B., Hood, R. W. & Gorsuch, R. L. (1985). *The psychology of religion: An empirical approach.* Englewood Cliffs, NJ: Prentice-Hall.

Stern, E. M. (Ed.). (1985). *Psychotherapy and the religiously committed patient.* New York: Haworth Press.

Strupp, H. H., & Hadley, S. M. (1977). A tripartite model of mental health and therapeutic outcomes. *American Psychologist, 32,* 187–196.

Walls, G. B. (1980). Values and psychotherapy: A comment on "Psychotherapy and Religious Values." *Journal of Consulting and Clinical Psychology, 48,* 640–641.

Wolpe, J. (1958). *Psychotherapy by reciprocal inhibition.* Stanford, CA: Stanford University Press.

Utilization of Spiritual Values in Counseling: An Ignored Dimension

ROBERT M. THEODORE

CARL ROGERS (1973) proposed the following:
> There may be a few who will dare to investigate the possibility that there is a lawful reality which is not open to our five senses; a reality in which present, past, and future are intermingled, in which space is not a barrier and time has disappeared . . . It is one of the most exciting challenges posed to psychology.

Rogers's statement underlies the basic tenet of this article. That is, if we can accept concepts such as self-worth, self-esteem, and self-actualization, if psychology finds these topics worthy of discussion, and if therapists can investigate these proposed constructs with their clients, then it is just as legitimate to explore the concept of spirituality.

The terms self-worth, self-esteem, and self-actualization are not tangible entities. No one can reach out and grab a piece of self-worth or scoop up a spoonful of self-actualization. In some of the relatively new theories, however, they are central themes that psychologists and counselors use freely in explaining personality deficiencies. It is common to speak of low self-esteem among delinquent adolescents or perhaps low self-worth in older women who are experiencing the "empty nest syndrome." Furthermore, attempts have been made to measure these characteristics in people. The Minnesota Multiphasic Personality Inventory (MMPI) or the 16 Personality Factors attempt to measure many human characteristics that reportedly exist. Still, the oldest of all human attributes, a feature that distinctly separates humans from earth's other creatures—spirituality—is a taboo for discussion. For some therapists (Ellis, 1962, 1980; Murray, 1974; Tholen, 1978) it is even something to be exorcised because they believe it is a form of emotional disorder.

Ellis (1962) hypothesized that "religiosity, to a large degree essentially is masochism, and both are forms of mental sickness." Ellis uses *Webster's New World Dictionary* to define religion as both belief in divine or superhuman power or powers to be obeyed and worshipped as the creator(s) and ruler(s) of the universe and expression of this belief in conduct and ritual. He contends that God should be "uninvented" and that belief in Him is irrational and a symptom of neurosis. Trying to help clients live effectively with and through their religion is the same as trying to help them live with emotional illness (Ellis, 1962, 1980). Therefore, the effective therapist must work with the client to oust irrational beliefs, that is, if the therapist "is not too sick or gutless to attack the client's religiosity" (Ellis, 1962). The issue is moderated and clarified in Ellis (1984), where only fanatic religionists are condemned, as are fanatic moralists or fanatic atheists.

Strong religious convictions are often condemned as being dogmatic and inflexible. As religious values are criticized and psychological values are espoused as more valid, however, what was flexible and liberal also tends to become dogmatic and absolutistic. That is, when psychology or a specific theory of psychology is touted as the only guiding light for living a healthy life, it becomes vulnerable to the same criticisms that have been hurled at religion. One can easily point out the dogmatic beliefs and ritualistic practices in psychotherapy. Such name calling is unproductive and in fact becomes humorous. It is quite similar to Abbott and Costello's arguing over who is on first. This argument will be more quickly resolved by empirical methods.

Ellis (1962) may be correct in saying that religion must be questioned but not thrown out. The empirical weapons of science can be used to bring out the useful aspects of religion (Bergin, 1980a; Walls, 1980). Current research exists in support of the contention that religion is beneficial to mental health (McClure & Loden, 1982; Shaver, Lenaur, & Sadd, 1980; Singh, 1979); others (Eron & Peterson, 1982) suggest no relationship between religiosity and measures of helping behavior. Ritzema (1979) critiques religious investigations and suggests topics for future research. The feud between psychology and religion requires resolution. An intensive empirical approach is the most effective and rational way to resolve the dispute.

Both Bergin (1980a) and Ellis (1980) suggest several hypotheses for scientific investigation (Table 1).

In denying spirituality as a legitimate part of life, psychologists are denying beliefs held by 90% of the U.S. population (Bergin, 1980a; Benson, 1981). It seems absurd if not unprofessional for mental health counselors to avoid the topic of religion when it has such a pervasive influence in American society. "Religion," according to a recent APA Monitor interview, "is the most important social force in the history of man...." Nevertheless, anyone trying to investigate religion is branded a meathead (Hogan, 1979, p. 4). When half this country is religiously oriented, it is unethical to avoid this consideration in psychotherapy (Cunningham, 1983). With so many people engaging in religious activities, it is probable that most clients seen in counseling have some religious values that influence their behavior. If the therapist does not integrate solutions that take into account spiritual or religious values into therapy, then effective outcomes will be temporary (Cunningham, 1983) or the benefits of therapy will be restricted (Lovinger, 1979).

Clients who present problems involving religious concerns are often referred to ministers or priests because a counselor (a) does not feel knowledgeable about religion, (b) belongs to a different religion, has none, or

TABLE 1
Testable Hypotheses From a Theistic and a Humanistic-Atheistic Frame of Reference

Theistic Hypothesis (Bergin, 1980, pp. 102–103)	Humanistic-Atheistic Hypothesis (Ellis, 1980, p. 638)
Religious communities that provide the combination of a viable belief structure and a network of loving, emotional support should manifest lower rates of emotional and social pathology and physical disease. Those who endorse high standards of impulse control (or strict moral standards) have lower than average rates of alcoholism, addiction, divorce, emotional instability, and associated interpersonal difficulties. Disturbances in clinical cases will diminish as these individuals are encouraged to adopt forgiving attitudes toward parents and others who may have had a part in the development of their symptoms. Infidelity or disloyalty to any interpersonal commitment, especially marriage, leads to harmful consequences—both interpersonally and intrapsychically. Teaching clients love, commitment, service, and sacrifice for others will help heal interpersonal difficulties and reduce intrapsychic distress. Improving male commitment, caring, and responsibility in families will reduce marital and familial conflict and associated psychological disorders. A good marriage and family life constitute a psychologically and socially benevolent state. As the percentage of persons in a community who live in such circumstances increases, social pathologies will decrease and vice versa. Properly understood, personal suffering can increase one's compassion and potential for helping others. The kinds of values described herein have social consequences. There is a social ecology, and the viability of this social ecology varies as a function of personal conviction, morality, and the quality of the social support network in which we exist.	Atheistic communities that provide a balanced, undogmatic belief structure and a cooperative, forgiving community without any absolutistic commandments will manifest lower rates of emotional, social pathology, and physical disease. Unequivocal and eternal fidelity or loyalty to any interpersonal commitment, especially marriage, leads to harmful consequences—both interpersonally and intrapsychically. Teaching clients forgiveness and selective love, commitment, service, and sacrifice for others will help heal interpersonal difficulties and reduce intrapsychic distress. Teaching them unselective, universal, and unequivocal love, commitment, service, and sacrifice for others will help sabotage interpersonal relations and increase intrapsychic distress. Personal suffering consisting of appropriate feelings like sorrow, regret, frustration, and annoyance at one's own or another's undesirable behavior will often increase one's compassion and potential for helping others. Personal suffering consisting of inappropriate feelings like panic, horror, depression, and hostility will usually decrease one's compassion and potential for helping others.

Note. From "Psychotherapy and Atheistic Values: A Response to A. E. Bergin's 'Psychotherapy and Religious Values' " by A. Ellis, 1980, *Journal of Consulting and Clinical Psychology, 48,* p. 638. Copyright 1980 by American Psychological Association. Adapted by permission.

(c) has negative beliefs about religion (Lovinger, 1979). These excuses are not adequate. Insufficient knowledge indicates a need for education. It is imperative that counselors keep expanding knowledge to serve clients. Most clients hold many beliefs and values that differ from the counselor's. If clients are to be rejected on religious grounds (either for the client's or the counselor's beliefs), perhaps they could be turned away for such other beliefs as the work ethic or lack of it, or marriage or not marrying. Clients come to therapy seeking help regarding their thoughts, behaviors, feelings, beliefs, and values. Religion is clearly an integral part of their value system and need not be feared.

Clients who express concerns in terms of religious rhetoric are expressing characterological problems given religious guise (Lovinger, 1979). The real concerns probably come from feelings such as guilt, remorse, or anger over some current or past behavior that may be tied to a religious value, but can be dealt with in much the same fashion as any other affective problem. For the client who insists on resisting therapy by putting up biblical blocks, Lovinger (1979) provides some excellent strategies for working through such problems. Other authors (Ellis, 1984; Hauck, 1972; Wessler, 1984) suggest methods that are effective in counseling clients with religiously related concerns.

A NEW MODEL FOR INCORPORATING SPIRITUALITY

Bergin (1980a) and Cunningham (1983) suggest the interaction of theistic values with humanistic idealism and clinical pragmatism to broaden clinical psychology's scope in relation to counseling and personality. To exclude spirituality is to refuse to look at a very significant influence on human behavior. Bergin (1980a) further suggests that part of the reason for the deterioration of society is a failure to recognize the important effect of God and religion on the lives of men and women. If psychologists insist on intervening on only the physical and the psychological characteristics of the client, then they are working only with the parts, not the whole. The whole human includes spirituality.

A more complete model of human behavior would look like the model in Figure 1. This model includes the three major aspects of human behavior. They intersect at the center. When the individual becomes unhealthy in any one of the three areas, the individual's system becomes unbalanced and the person develops certain symptoms that identify the problem area. When well-being has been regained, the person again becomes centered and each of the systems functions appropriately. Good balance may be defined as the level of functioning at which individuals feel comfortable and are considered healthy for themselves and for society. The level of functioning may change with age or educational perspective. That is, at different times of life, one

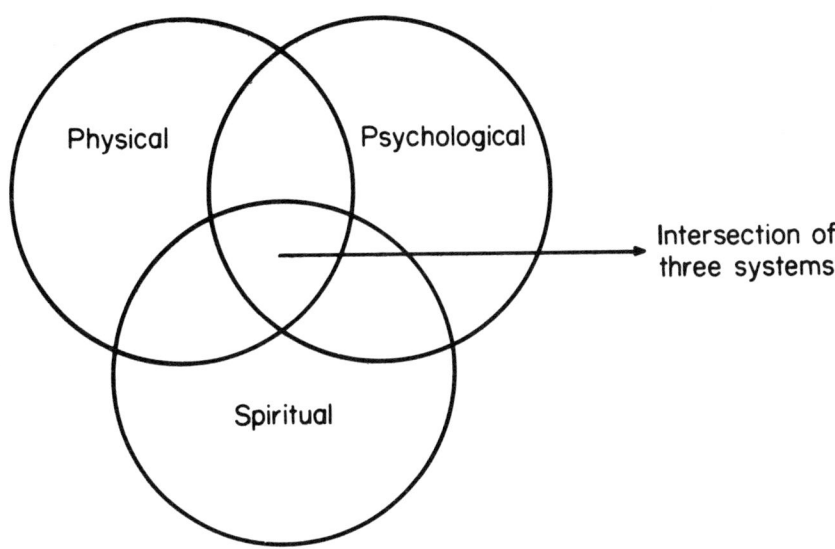

FIGURE 1
A Model of the Three Major Characteristics of Human Behavior

part of the system will be more important than another, based on one's perceived need or cognition set at a particular time in life.

Therapists who refuse to accept spirituality as part of the human makeup, says Bergin (1980a), should tell that to their clients. This would show proper respect for the clients' values. Furthermore, if therapists and counselors hold values sufficiently different from the client population, "it would be ethical to publicize where we stand." Then people would not be deceived (Bergin, 1980a; Ellis, 1980). Other therapists propose that it is unethical to avoid spiritual issues in therapy (Cunningham, 1983) because religious belief and activity is so pervasive.

SUMMARY

It has been the intent of this article to encourage counselors to be sensitive to a client's religious background and accompanying personal values (Cunningham, 1983; Bergin, 1980a, 1980b; Lovinger, 1979) and to explore these spiritual attitudes and feelings to relieve psychic suffering. It is not the counselor's role to replace the client's point of view with another but to integrate theistic reasoning with solutions to produce stable, effective, and lasting results.

Furthermore, it is strongly suggested that the bickering over which system of values is most effective be stopped and a productive scientific approach be adopted. Bergin (1980a) and Ellis (1980) suggest some researchable hypotheses, whereas Ritzema (1979) proposes methods and topics. Finally, counselors are urged to learn about religious values in order to more effectively serve their predominantly religious clientele.

REFERENCES

Benson, J. M. (1981). The polls: A rebirth of religion. *Public Opinion Quarterly, 45,* 576–585.

Bergin, A. E. (1980a). Psychotherapy and religious values. *Journal of Consulting and Clinical Psychology, 48,* 95–104.

Bergin, A. E. (1980b). Religious and humanistic values: A reply to Ellis and Walls. *Journal of Consulting and Clinical Psychology, 48,* 642–645.

Cunningham, S. (1983, December). Spirituality seen as neglected aspect of psychotherapy. *APA Monitor,* p. 21.

Ellis, A. (1962, October). The case against religion: A psychotherapist's view. *The Independent,* pp. 1–7.

Ellis, A. (1980). Psychotherapy and atheistic values. A response to A. E. Bergin's "Psychotherapy and religious values." *Journal of Consulting and Clinical Psychology, 48,* 635–639.

Ellis, A. (1984). Rational emotive therapy (RET) and pastoral counseling: A reply to Richard Wessler. *Personnel and Guidance Journal, 62,* 266–267.

Eron, L., & Peterson, R. A. (1982). Abnormal behavior: Social approaches. *Annual Review of Psychology, 33,* 231–264.

Hauck, P. A. (1972). *Reason in pastoral counseling.* Philadelphia: Westminster.

Hogan, R. (1979, April). Interview. *APA Monitor,* pp. 4–5.

Lovinger, R. J. (1979). Therapeutic strategies with religious resistances. *Psychotherapy: Theory, Research and Practice, 16,* 419–427.

McClure, R. F., & Loden, M. (1982). Religious activity, denomination, membership and life satisfaction. *Psychology: A Quarterly Journal of Human Behavior, 19,* 12–17.

Murray, M. (1974). *Why I am an atheist.* Austin, TX: American Atheist Press.

Ritzema, R. J. (1979). Religiosity and altruism: Faith without works. *Journal of Theology and Psychology, 7,* 105–113.

Rogers, C. (1973). Some new challenges. *American Psychologist, 28,* 379–387.

Shaver, P., Lenaur, M., & Sadd, S. (1980). Religiousness, conversion, and subjective well-being: The "healthy minded" religion of modern American women. *American Journal of Psychiatry, 137,* 1563–1568.

Singh, A. (1979). Religious involvement and antisocial behavior. *Perceptual and Motor Skills, 48,* 1157–1158. (From *Psychological Abstracts,* 1979, 61, No. 12724.)

Tholen, G. (1978). More psychiatric implications of religion. *American Atheist, 20,* 15.

Walls, G. B. (1980). Values and psychotherapy: A comment on "Psychotherapy and religious values." *Journal of Consulting and Clinical Psychology, 48,* 640–641.

Wessler, R. L. (1984). A bridge too far: Incompatibilities of rational emotive therapy and pastoral counseling. *Personnel and Guidance Journal, 62,* 264–265.

The Counselor and Religious Dilemma: A Personal Experience

C. EDWARD WATKINS, JR.

"You see, I just need to learn to depend on God, to quit worrying about my life and put it all in His hands. If I could just do that, everything would take care of itself."

I felt my body tighten as Bill, a student client, expressed his desire to become more trusting of God's will for his life. I was touched by and saddened for him, for I knew he was locked in a deep personal struggle, a struggle that could potentially shake him to the very core of his being.

I tried to overcome the tightness I experienced; the feeling was inhibiting me from listening fully to Bill, and I strongly wanted to hear what he had to say. As I thought of his "need to learn to depend on God," however, I was flooded by a sea of personal memories, some bitter and some sweet, that swept me away to a not so distant time when I experienced a similar religious struggle of my own. I remember speaking those words, for at one time I had felt the pull to lose myself entirely in what I thought was the mystical external God. I wanted to be totally and completely immersed in a religion or way of being that seemed right. I needed structure and strived desperately to obtain it. But the structure always seemed tenuous, fabricated; it was never satisfying or comforting.

And this is what Bill wanted—the structure of God to order his life. He repeated time and time again that all of his problems were cause by an inability to let go, to give everything up to God. His words continually touched off remembrances and feelings within me I had not experienced vividly for some time, and I grew vexed and irritated with myself for not being able to better attend. I felt so strongly for him: His tears and doubts were mine; his terrible confusion and desperation I had experienced. I so wanted to help him, to prevent in some way this awful struggle he was embroiled in. But I knew I could not. I knew I could not stop his turmoil, no matter how much I would like to. The struggle was deeply and personally his; he would have to arrive at his own resolution, and I knew the process of resolving would be both painful and tumultuous.

I felt helpless and powerless in the wake of his agitation. I thought I could at least listen and try to understand, let him know there was someone interested in his welfare, someone who would be there with him throughout this ordeal. But I wondered, too, if I could really do these things; that is, could I truly listen to and understand his concerns? Would I not be hampered by my own over-identification with him? How could I be effective if I were constantly besieged by past personal preoccupations?

Bill's turmoil was visibly evident: The tears were large and heavy in his eyes, and his face was suffused with terror and despair. There was a real sense of urgency to this counseling session for him. He needed answers immediately, but also recognized that I did not possess the truth he was in search of. If ever there had been a time when I would like to have known the truth or possessed all of the answers to religious dilemma, this would have been it. I would have enjoyed easing and eliminating his pain—oh, to have seen a smile crease his face. But there were no smiles, and there were no pills or panaceas I had to offer. There were only he and I, together, locked in a bitter struggle to know, to gain knowledge into Self. And this was not a struggle he had requested; rather, it was one forced upon him as a participant in life. It was, to use an existentialist term, a given.

I became aware of a strong sense of awkwardness in working with Bill, an awkwardness compounded by the fact that he now wanted to adopt a way of being I had totally rejected. I could not accept being immersed in a religious system that seemed to deprive people of freedom, autonomy, and actualization. Neither could I accept Bill's desire to become completely consumed by a rigidly structured, definite do/definite do not type of theology. I wanted desperately, though, to work with him, feel with him, and, yes, even suffer with him.

One question continually confronted me, however: Could I defer my personal opinions and slants enough to assist him? I wanted to help in some way, however minor it might be, but in all honesty I was not sure if I could. My past experiences and old familiar feelings kept resurfacing in the interview, and I was at a loss as to how I could suppress them. I wasn't even sure I wanted to suppress these feelings, because they were truly me, truly part of the person I had become.

The internal polarities I felt left me confused and indecisive. I wondered if Bill was aware of my personal discord; he didn't seem to be, for he continued to express his distress and inner trepidation. He was hurting badly, and coming to talk with me provided him an opportunity to ease his burden. Nevertheless, I knew that if I did not begin to tie in with his experience more, I could lose him, and that was something I definitely did not want to do.

I doggedly pushed my preoccupations aside and began to focus in on his verbalizations. I listened with intensity and feeling, yet it was difficult not to be lured away by personal opinion and conviction. But I was determined to salvage this relationship. Bill needed me, and, to some extent, I am sure I needed him. And with my resolve came a greater involvement and understanding. I listened intently to what he had to say; I reflected his thoughts and feelings, and he knew I was really with him.

His puzzlement and deep despair soon gave way to an oppressed lightness. He joked some, but yet seemed very introspective and examining. His contemplations were somber and quiet, highly personalistic and meaningful. He struggled with the religious dilemma that confronted him, but he knew regardless of the outcome that I cared about him and that I was involved and invested in his welfare.

At this point, I could not help but be struck by the immense irony and humor of the situation. I recognized that Bill and I were vastly different and, too, that we were startlingly alike. We had traveled similar paths and had perhaps felt kin agonies, desperations, and ecstacies. We were brothers, but also aliens. We deeply cared for one another, and yet could simultaneously hate and despise each other. There was unity between us and, saddeningly, a fragmentation.

I could not help but wonder how this first session would end. I so hoped we would continue working together; I was sure Bill wanted that, and I knew I did, too. Together, we had covered a vast amount of territory—he had talked, and I had listened. I was happy with how I had been able to put aside my own religious biases enough so that I could understand and, to some degree, promote Bill's understanding of himself. It had not been easy to subordinate personal conviction, but I felt that I had. From my perspective, I had overcome self to be of assistance to another, and although the struggle had indeed been difficult, I was pleased with my effort.

I noticed that Bill had stopped talking now and was staring down at the floor. He seemed quite pensive, and subsequently began fidgeting in his chair. He quickly advanced a thoughtful glance toward me and then, once again, looked downward. I got the distinct impression he wanted to ask me something, something that weighed heavily on his mind, but I was not sure. Precious minutes passed by; nothing of substance was said. And then, as our interview was coming to a close, Bill looked at me with great hesitation and caution and asked the questions I did not anticipate, questions that indicated that perhaps my suppression of bias and attitude had not been as successful as I had thought.

"Sir," he queried curiously, "do you believe in God? Are you a Christian?"

The Moral Nature of Psychotherapy

BARRY GRANT

MOST PSYCHOTHERAPISTS TODAY no longer naively believe that psychotherapy is a value-free enterprise. Most will acknowledge that buried under talk about theory, research, techniques, strategies, legal concerns, and professional images are values and moral positions. For this awareness, therapists are indebted to a number of books and articles written since the 1940s that argue for an image of psychotherapy as a fundamentally moral enterprise (e.g., Bergin, 1980; Green, 1946; Jahoda, 1958; London, 1964; Lowe, 1959; Smith, 1961; Strupp, 1980; Szasz, 1978; Watson, 1958; Weisskopf-Joelson, 1980). Yet, although psychotherapists know that psychotherapy is not value-free, they do not seem to have given much attention to the values inherent in their practice (Van Hoose & Kottler, 1977), nor do they fully appreciate the extent to which moral values are imbedded in the psychotherapeutic enterprise. London (1964) describes a state of affairs that, to all appearances, has remained unchanged 20 years later.

> ... psychotherapeutic training programs in psychiatry, psychology, social work—even in the ministry—often do not deal seriously with the problem of morals. Psychotherapeutic literature is full of formal principles of procedures and somewhat vague statements of goals, but it generally says little or nothing about the possible moral implications of these procedures and goals—indeed, it often fails even to mention that there are any moral, as opposed to scientific, implications to psychotherapy, though the objectives of the latter are rationalized by the former. It is as if therapists were themselves unconscious of some of the most profound difficulties in their own work. (p. 6)

The image of psychotherapy as a fundamentally moral enterprise does not seem to be deeply rooted in the consciousness of psychotherapists. Psychotherapists typically see themselves as applied scientists whose main task is developing and using techniques and technologies to get a job done. They seldom ask whether the job should be done and what the morally good ways of accomplishing it are.

When therapists put aside their preoccupation with theoretical and technical matters and explicitly consider the moral aspects of their practice, they tend to treat moral concerns as a subdivision of practice, not as the ground of practice. They encapsulate them as separate and distinct from what they consider to be purely psychotherapeutic concerns. They professionalize moral issues so that they enter practice and thinking primarily by way of professional and legal issues and problem situations closely tied to these issues (e.g., conflicts between maintaining client confidentiality and protecting the safety of others), and by way of concerns with professional competence, the advancement of the aims of the profession, and the maintenance of the good graces of society.

The importance psychotherapists give to moral concerns can most easily be seen in psychotherapy and counseling texts. The ratio of the number of pages in which moral values or cognate terms are mentioned to the total pages of a sample of recent texts are as follows: Basch (1980), 0/180; Bell (1975), 5/389; Brammer and Shostrom (1982), 40/437; Cormier and Cormier (1977), 10/517; Corsini (1979), 0/535; Haley (1976), 27/268; Korchin (1976), 5/608; Kottler (1983), 18/295; Krumboltz and Thoresen (1976), 9/565; Martin (1983), 7/272; Pietrofesa, Hoffman, and Splete (1984), 17/515; Shulman (1979), 0/354. The sample is nonrepresentative (and the measure is rough) but it suggests forcibly that moral values are not considered greatly important to the teaching and practice of psychotherapy.

There is, then, still a point to presenting additional arguments for psychotherapy as moral enterprise. This article attempts to substantiate and elaborate the claim that moral values (*not* psychological theory, research, or the best interests of the profession) are the necessary ground of psychotherapeutic practice.

MORAL ENTERPRISES AND MORAL VALUES

The argument that psychotherapy is a moral enterprise presupposes an image of human life, a notion of a moral enterprise drawn from this image, and a particular conception of moral values. It has its sense and force in the context of these assumptions. Any conception of the place of morality in psychotherapy must be tied to conceptions of the nature of human beings and on the other hand to a conception of the nature of morality. I have endeavored to define both points very broadly. The image of human beings presented here is very common among Westerners and constitutes the assumption needed to make talk about morality meaningful at all. Briefly, I assume that human beings have agency, that they make decisions, choose courses of actions based on their decisions, and have responsibility for their actions. Human enterprises are comprised of actions; actions are chosen based on decisions; decisions are based on reasons or values. A moral enterprise is an enterprise based implicitly or explicitly on moral reasons or values.

Moral values cannot be easily defined because morality itself, upon which a definition of a moral value depends, cannot be defined easily or at all. The reason for this is largely historical. We are, as MacIntyre (1966, 1981) has shown, the inheritors of a motley incommensurable lot of moralities and moral discourses. Kantians, Marxists, Christians, Utilitarians, Wittgensteinians, Buddhists, and Rationalists, for example, each advance different and many incompatible claims about the nature of morality and its claims on us.

In spite of the problems arising from disagreements about the nature of morality, it is possible to establish a clear, objective, general definition of the domain of moral values that captures a central element of most, but not all moralities. (Excluded, I think, are only egoistic moral theories and moral theories that place the locus of morality in man's relationship to God or an absolute.) Values are preferences and desires for, and attributions of meaning and worth to, states of affairs or courses of actions (cf. Kluckhohn, 1951). Values are an actual or possible attitude of a human subject to the world as he or she experiences it.

Moral values are distinguished from values in general in that they encompass only attitudes towards other individuals and attitudes towards actions that affect them. More specifically, *moral values* are attitudes regarding and actions affecting their well-being. These attitudes are expressed in the many forms of moral discourse and morality, in talk about love, rights, responsibilities, duties, compassion, moral goodness, and benevolence. Different moralities prescribe and proscribe different behaviors, give different justifications for moral actions, and have different conceptions of well-being, but all have as their reason for being a concern for the well-being of others. Morality would not matter if the welfare of others did not matter.

It should be understood that the word "moral," when referring to enterprises and values, has as its opposite "nonmoral" not "immoral": It describes a class of values, not as an appraisal of a value. To argue that psychotherapy is a moral enterprise, then, is not to give wholesale approval to every psychotherapeutic practice; rather, the argument refocuses discussion, criticism, and justification of therapeutic practices. This argument is a necessary preliminary to the task of providing a particular moral basis for psychotherapy.

The notions of human agency, moral enterprise, and moral values are the tacit assumptions of the central portion of the article. Two delineations of the relationships among three elements of psychotherapy—theory (including facts), moral values, and actual practice (cf. London, 1964)—are presented. Because therapists typically justify and guide their practice by reference to theory, the theoretical component of psychotherapy receives the most attention in both arguments. The moral nature of psychotherapy can be demonstrated most instructively by examining the most common basis of practice. I hope to show that, on one view, theory cannot be the basis of practice but that moral values must be, and that, on another view, moral values (the basis of practice) are embodied in theory.

THEORIES AS REPRESENTATIONAL

Edwards (1982), following the work of Wittgenstein, describes a conception of rationality he calls "rationality-as-representation": thought, rationality, as a means for achieving accurate, true representations of the world. Rationality-as-representation is a form of thinking reflected in the common notion that truth consists in getting the world right and in representing reality correctly. Science is generally considered to be the font of truths about the way the world is. These truths are given in the form of propositions that represent the world. Propositions are either factual or theoretical. Facts are states of affairs, actual or hypothetical. Factual propositions are linguistic representations of facts (i.e., pictures of facts). "The pot is on the fire," pictures some actual or hypothetical pot on a fire. True factual propositions represent actual facts. Theories are explanatory propositions (Marx, 1976) that represent a relationship between facts. They are pictures of pictures or facts about facts. Theories represent superordinate or higher level facts not necessarily more or less true or provisional than the facts they picture. "Facts are small theories and true theories are big facts" (Goodman, 1978, p. 97).

In order for psychotherapy or any enterprise to be free of values, including moral values, it must be based entirely on representations of the way the world is (i.e., on factual propositions and theories). This follows directly from the definitions of facts, theories, and values. What else could a value-free enterprise be based on than, by definition, an absence of values? We free ourselves from values by sticking just to the facts, and we get and verify the facts primarily by doing science. Through the methods of science, we are able to achieve true representations of the way the world is.

The impossibility of basing any enterprise just on true factual propositions and true theories is immediately obvious. Indeed, the notion of a value-free enterprise has never meant that the process of finding facts and developing theories is value free. It means, rather, that the facts and theories resulting from the process are value free. The process, the enterprise itself, requires at least the values of attribution of worth to particular lines of inquiry and an interest in the topic. In the sense in which "enterprise" is used here, neither science, nor psychotherapy, nor any other enterprise can be value-free.

Facts as facts and theories as big facts cannot constitute a reason for acting. Neither can function alone as reasons for making choices, except as they are understood as elliptical for values. It is nonsense to have as a reason for going to the store, "there is bread at the store" (fact), unless it is assumed that bread is in some way valued. It is nonsense to have as a reason for interpreting transference in psychoanalysis, "interpreting transferences is necessary to curing neuroses" (theory), unless it is understood that some value is attached to curing neuroses. These are common sorts of reasons, and in most instances they are meaningful because the ellipsis is either assumed or made obvious by the context of the remark; unless they are understood to imply values, however, such reasons are nonsense.

Factual propositions and theories cannot function as reasons for actions and they cannot be the basis of an enterprise because they have no necessary implication for practice. Unless we desire or attribute worth to the states of affairs they depict, they stand before us as inert and impotent data. If one is hungry (fact) and there is bread at the store (fact), one has no basis for seeking the bread unless one makes a judgment about the respective values of remaining hungry and of troubling to go to the store. Similarly, if one grants that Freud was right about humans, it does not necessarily follow then that one should practice psychotherapy as Freud did any more than it follows that one should lobotomize one's clients, let them stew in their juices, or prescribe rest cures in the Alps for them. Even when all the known facts are woven together with a theory, one still does not have any prescription for what to do.

An evaluation of facts and of possible actions (possible future facts) is a necessary basis for action. From only a superficial rendering of the psychotherapeutic enterprise, one can see that the values necessary to determine a course of action in psychotherapy must be moral values. A common element of all psychotherapies is that psychotherapy both affects the well-being of individuals in psychotherapy and has their well-being as an overriding focus. This is implicit in Frank's (1963) characterization of psychotherapy as including a healer, a sufferer, and a series of structured contacts between the two. This is stated explicitly by Watson (1958) who writes, "Psychotherapy endeavors to make lost, unhappy, and unproductive people able to lead more meaningful, more useful, and more satisfying lives. This is in itself a highly ethical undertaking" (p. 574).

Harm or good can be done in any human relationships not just in psychotherapy (Temaner, 1977). Inherent characteristics of the psychotherapeutic relationship, however, place a special moral responsibility on the therapist (Temaner, 1977). This additional responsibility derives from the inherent inequality of power in the therapy relationship: The therapist as the helpgiver possesses more power than the client or clients who receive help. To the client, the therapist is also a trusted, perhaps wise, confidant with special skills and expertise who matters a great deal. The therapist has potentially great impact for good or ill on the client's well-being. The therapist's use of power has potentially great and far-reaching consequences. Temaner (1977) writes,

> The therapist has a special responsibility to be effective and responsible for [his or her actions and cannot] necessarily say, 'I am a therapist, I help people,' because being a therapist simply puts one in a position of being able to do a great deal of harm or good—depending. (p. 2)

THEORIES AS PRAGMATIC AND VALUE-LADEN

A conception of theories and facts as representing the way things are presupposes a distinction between the world and ways of looking at the world. Goodman (1978), Rorty (1982), and Edwards (1982), among others, have argued against a view of rationality that requires this dichotomy. Goodman (1978) puts the point this way:

> If I ask about the world, you can offer to tell me how it is under one or more frames of reference; but if I insist that you tell me how it is apart from all frames, what can you say? We are confined to ways of describing whatever is described. Our universe, so to speak, consists of these ways rather than of a world or of worlds. (pp. 2–3)

On this view, the world is a way of describing the world. Differences among versions of the world replace the difference between the world and representations of it necessary to the representational view of theory. Theories and facts are true only in relationship to other versions of the world, and the question of whether they get the world right does not arise.

The way the world is is made by us in many different ways according to our uses and purposes. We make facts and theories and we make ourselves and our worlds with them.

Theories may still *function* as representations of the world. We may take them and use them as pictures of the world, but their value lies not in their accuracy, which we can only assess indirectly and hypothetically by how well they work. Rather, their value lies in how well they help us function in the world and in the value of the world in which they help us function.

Theories, because they are human creations, must be made on the basis of particular values, preferences, and conceptions of a good life, however inchoate these might be. Theories are also the result of many decisions on how to look at and study the world; these decisions are made by estimating the relative worth of one view over another. Theories embody and express the values that directed their development. Just as a work of art embodies the relative value given to line, form, color, subject, and method in the creation of the work, so theories embody the value given to methods of study, modes of explanation, subject matter, and image of human being (Gergen, 1980). Skinnerian theory, for example, clearly shows a valuing of a deterministic view of behavior, a positivist conception of science, observable phenomena, and precise, quantifiable data. Theorists, like artists, use their creative apprehension to express and represent the world in a multitude of forms.

Theories can and should be judged on the basis of how well they enable us to accomplish ends we wish to accomplish, of whether we want to live in a world populated by the sorts of humans they describe, and of whether we value the goals, opportunities, ways of relating to each other, and life projects the theories make possible. We can and do judge, for example, whether the views on human beings offered by Freud, Skinner, Ellis, and Rogers are good ones.

Psychological theories function as values in research and psychotherapy in the same way that religious creeds, political philosophies, and artistic doctrines function in their respective domains. Values are not needed to mediate between theory and action for this conception of theory as they were in the view of theory presented earlier. Theory can function as a basis for action and it does have necessary implications for practice. To act on the basis of a theory is to act on values. Freudian theory, for example, is an adequate basis for analyzing transferences because the good of doing so is written into the theory: the theory prescribes certain action and proscribes others.

Psychotherapy, from the pragmatic view of theory, is necessarily a moral enterprise. In their origin, substance, and use theories are value laden. The values function as moral values in the context of psychotherapy because they are the basis for action that affects the well-being of the client. Most theories also provide the definition of what counts as well-being. The choice and use of a theory, then, is a moral act because it is at the same time a choice and excercise of values.

The choice of a theory is also a moral choice on the representational view. No psychological theory is in any position to be declared more accurate than any other (London, 1964). There are no compelling grounds for choosing Freud's theory over Roger's, or Skinner's over Perls's on the basis of their verisimilitude, nor is there agreement on how to assess accuracy of representation. Because the choice matters a great deal to how the therapist acts in therapy, views what is possible or impossible for clients, and conceptualizes well-being, the choice is a moral choice.

IMPLICATIONS

This article has presented two distinct conceptions of theories and facts, of the relationship of theories and facts to values, and of psychotherapy as a moral enterprise. In each case the practice of psychotherapy necessarily rests on moral values. These values are either explicitly stated or tacitly assumed, or they are embodied in and expressed through the use of theory. Theory, because of its important place in psychotherapy, has received considerable attention. It is, however, in the nature of psychotherapy not of theory, that psychotherapy is a moral enterprise. Psychotherapy in its necessary concern with, and great potential for affecting, the well-being of others is an inherently ethical enterprise.

It is not enough for therapists to just see that they are engaged in a moral enterprise. A brief moment of perception followed by a resumption of the same quality of activity is a fruitless consequence of awareness. A conception of psychotherapy as a moral enterprise necessarily requires modifications in the training of psychotherapists and in the justification and presentation of forms of psychotherapy. Moral concerns, issues, and philosophies should be the primary focus with theoretical and technical matters secondary. Moral issues should not be shunted off to the periphery of practice, but should be recognized as present in every therapeutic intervention. Interpreting transferences, self-disclosing, giving advice, empathizing, and giving paradoxical directives are moral acts, and questions of whether and when to engage in them are moral questions: Each can and does affect clients' well-being, for better or for worse.

As London (1964) noted in the passage above, both the procedures and goals of psychotherapy have moral implications. Well-being is affected not only by the ends achieved by the therapist's actions but also by the means used to achieve the ends. Means have effects independent of the ends that partially define the ends. A symptom relieved through insight is a different state of affairs then one extinguished through lack of reinforcement. Morally good practice, then, is not equivalent to practice that serves morally good goals. Equating good practice with seeking good goals obscures the intimate, subtle relationships between the therapist's exercise of power and authority and its effects on clients' well-being and it ignores the more difficult matter of establishing and justifying the moment-to-moment means to these goals. Professional ethical standards such as the American Psychological Association "Principles" (1981) and American Personnel and Guidance Association "Standards" (1974) are too vague, broad, and superficial to offer the necessary moral justification and guidance. Worse yet, they mislead therapists and the public into believing that adherence to the principles will yield morally good practice. Adherence to professional standards cannot insure morally good practice because they are inadequate and fail to come to grips with the moral heart of psychotherapy.

To the extent that demonstrations of the moral nature of psychotherapy remain scattered or incomplete and the moral nature of psychotherapy is ignored or denied, psychotherapy clients are treated as means not ends, as objects, and as instruments for self-aggrandizement and self-satisfaction. This is not an unfair, exaggerated claim about the moral character of therapists as a group, but merely an implication of the fact that we human beings almost always deny moral status to things and sometimes to animals, and treat them either as opportunities for exercising our will or as means to ends.

We may be forgiven moral lapses in our everyday behavior. We may even be forgiven them at those times when, because our power to affect others is great, our responsibility to act well is great. But, we cannot be forgiven for failing to attempt to think through and justify our actions once we are aware of their moral nature or for trying to fulfill our responsibilities and act well as we perceive acting well, fail though we might.

Undoubtedly, if the implications of psychotherapy as a moral enterprise were taken seriously, the diversity of views regarding the moral basis of psychotherapy, its relationship to theory and practice, and the nature of morally good practice would be as great as any current diversity of opinion in the field of psychotherapy. But at least the disagreement would be in the right place.

REFERENCES

American Personnel and Guidance Association. (1974). *Ethical Standards*. Falls Church, VA: Author.

Basch, M. F. (1980). *Doing psychotherapy*. New York: Basic Books.

Bell, J. B. (1975). *Family therapy*. New York: Jason Aronson.

Bergin, A. E. (1980). Psychotherapy and religious values. *Psychotherapy: Theory, Research, and Practice, 17*(4), 95–105.

Brammer, L. M. & Shostrom, E. L. (1982). *Therapeutic psychology: Fundamentals of counseling and psychotherapy*. Englewood Cliffs, NJ: Prentice-Hall.

Cormier, W. H., & Cormier, L. S. (1977). *Interview strategies for helpers: A guide to assessment, treatment, and evaluation.* Monterey, CA: Brooks/Cole.

Corsini, R. J. (1979). *Current psychotherapies.* Itasca, IL: Peacock.

Edwards, J. C. (1982). *Ethics without philosophy: Wittgenstein and the moral life.* Tampa: University Presses of Florida.

Ethical principles of psychologists. (1981). *American Psychologist, 36,* 633–638.

Frank, J. D. (1963). *Persuasion and healing.* New York: Schoken.

Gergen, K. J. (1980). The emerging crisis in life-span developmental theory. In P. B. Baltes, & O. G. Brim, (Eds.), *Life span development and behavior* (Vol. 3). New York: Academic Press.

Goodman, N. (1978). *Ways of worldmaking.* Indianapolis: Hackett.

Green, A. W. (1946). Social values and psychotherapy. *Journal of Personality, 14*(3), 199–228.

Haley, J. (1976). *Problem solving therapy.* New York: Harper & Row.

Jahoda, M. (1958). *Current concepts of positive mental health.* New York: Basic Books.

Kluckhohn, C. K. M. (1951). Values and value orientations in the theory of action. In T. Parsons & A. E. Shils (Eds.), *Toward a general theory of action.* (pp. 388–433). Cambridge, MA: Harvard University Press.

Korchin, S. J. (1976). *Modern clinical psychology: Principles of intervention in the clinic and community.* New York: Basic Books.

Kottler, J. A. (1983). *Pragmatic group leadership.* Monterey, CA: Brooks/Cole.

Krumboltz, J. D., & Thoresen, L. E. (1976). *Counseling methods.* New York: Holt, Rinehart and Winston.

London, P. (1964). *The modes and morals of psychotherapy.* New York: Holt, Rinehart, and Winston.

Lowe, C. M. (1959). Value orientations—An ethical dilemma. *American Psychologist, 14*(10), 687–693.

MacIntyre, A. (1966). *A short history of ethics.* New York: MacMillan.

MacIntyre, A. (1981). *After virtue: A study in moral theory.* Notre Dame: University of Notre Dame Press.

Martin, D. G. (1983). *Counseling and therapy skills.* Monterey, CA: Brooks/Cole.

Marx, M. H. (1976). Formal theory. In M. H. Marx & F. E. Goodson (Eds.), *Theories in contempory psychology* (pp. 239–252). New York: Macmillan.

Pietrofesa, J. J., Hoffman, A., & Splete, H. H. (1984). *Counseling: An introduction.* Boston: Houghton Mifflin.

Rorty, R. (1982). *Consequences of pragmatism.* Minneapolis: University of Minnesota.

Shulman, L. (1979). *The skills of helping individuals and groups.* Itasca, IL: Peacock.

Smith, M. B. (1961). Mental health reconsidered: A special case of the problem of values in psychology. *American Psychologist, 16*(6), 299–306.

Strupp, H. H. (1980). Humanism and psychotherapy: A personal statement of the therapist's essential values. *Psychotherapy: Theory, Research, and Practice, 17*(4), 396–400.

Szasz, T. (1978). *The myth of psychotherapy: Mental healing as religion, rhetoric, and repression.* Garden City, NY: Anchor Press.

Temaner, B. (1977). *Ethics in psychotherapy.* Unpublished manuscript.

Van Hoose, W. H., & Kottler, J. A. (1977). *Ethical and legal issues in counseling and psychotherapy.* San Francisco: Jossey Bass.

Watson, G. (1958). Moral issues in psychotherapy. *American Psychologist, 13*(9), 574–576.

Weisskopf-Joelson, E. (1980). Values: The *enfant terrible* of psychotherapy. *Psychotherapy: Theory, Research and Practice, 17*(4), 459–466.

The Morality of Influencing in Counseling

JOHN M. SCHULTE

IN THIS ANALYSIS I identify a number of factors that I believe any counselor must consider in assessing the morality of his or her influences on clients. My analysis is predicated on several assumptions about the nature of morality and the connections between morality and the actions of counselors. In this limited context, I can neither explicate them fully nor give them adequate justification. I will simply list them with brief comments:

1. Values, including moral values, are inevitably embedded in the counseling process. Values held by a counselor will inevitably influence his or her counseling decisions and actions. Value neutrality is an impossibility. Many authorities have offered strong arguments for this position; for example, London (1964), Lowe (1976), Breggin (1971), Macklin (1973), Karasu (1980), and Bergin (1985).

2. There are important connections between morality and rationality. Determining what is morally right often requires serious deliberation. One cannot count on laws, customs, institutional policies, or one's personal feelings to establish what is moral. This position, as well as No. 3 and No. 4, are rooted in the philosophy of Immanuel Kant and other *deontological* theorists who followed him. A full discussion of this viewpoint is offered by Baier (1965). The implications of this viewpoint for counseling are discussed by Carroll, Schneider, and Wesley (1985).

3. Moral decisions and actions are justified by reference to moral principles and rules that take precedence over the individual's wants and desires if they come into conflict with them. Many contemporary moral theorists have provided explication and justification for this position; for example, Fried (1970), Peters (1974), Brody (1970), Gert (1973).

4. Respect for persons is the fundamental moral principle and the basis for other moral principles that establish basic moral obligations for human interactions: to achieve maximum freedom, to be truthful, to consider the interests of all affected parties, and to treat persons impartially. This position has received much attention in philosophical literature over a long period of time. Examples: MacLagan (1960), Downie and Telfer (1969).

5. The application of moral principles and rules to specific situations can be extremely complex as, for example, when circumstances bring two principles in conflict. Reasoning is an indispensable tool for dealing with moral

problems but is not so effective that it can resolve all problems. There are, and will probably always be, plenty of moral dilemmas and issues about which reasoning persons will disagree.

6. Widespread public discussion of moral problems, alternative courses of action to deal with them, and justification of alternative actions is essential for societal and professional moral growth. Many authorities in the field of counseling apparently share assumptions No. 5 and No. 6. See, for example, Peterson (1976), Edward (1982), and Rosenbaum (1982). I hope that this analysis also illustrates the complexity of moral reasoning and will contribute to the public discussion of moral problems.

A MATRIX OF INFLUENCE

Influence is a concept of extremely broad application. People influence one another in a host of different ways. Sometimes influencing is overt, as in persuasion; sometimes it is covert, as in guilt manipulation. Sometimes the influencer is doing it on purpose; sometime it is unintentional. The results of influencing can be beneficial, harmful, or both.

Analyzing the morality of influencing on a case by case basis would be a long and involved process. Perhaps the process can be compressed by formulating a matrix of influencing. All cases of influencing in human contexts seem to have the following features:

1. *An influencer* (or *influencers*), the person or persons doing the influencing, henceforth referred to as *I*
2. *The receiver* (or *receivers*) of the influence; the person or persons subject to the influence, henceforth referred to as *R*
3. A *change* in behavior, belief, attitude, feeling, or disposition that the influence contributes to or discourages, henceforth referred to as *C*
4. *The means* of influencing; the particular things that *I* does or says that influence *R*, henceforth referred to as *M*

These factors can be put together to form a matrix of all cases of influencing in human contexts, as follows: *I* contributes to (or helps to prevent) *C* in *R* by means *M*.

To avoid confusion, it is important to note the following about the use of the matrix in analysis.

1. Clearly, the *I*, the influencer, can be one person, a group of persons, like an ethical standards committee, or even a large amorphous group like a corporation. Our concern, however, is the morality of influencing done by counselors, so we will only consider cases in which the *I* is one person.

2. The term *means* is somewhat misleading. It seems to suggest that whatever an *I* does to influence an *R*, he or she does it deliberately. People choose various means to accomplish their objectives. As I will discuss later, however, many acts of influence are unintentional. In this analysis *M*, or means, is used to refer to both intentional and unintentional acts of influencing.

This matrix tells nothing about the morality or immorality of influencing, but it may be useful in helping to identify morally relevant factors in cases in which one person is influencing others. In the next section, I will consider each of the components of the matrix in turn and try to establish the relevant factors for determining whether the actions of *I*, the influencer, are moral or immoral.

To be helpful to the reader, I will reverse the usual order of things by presenting the conclusions first and then the discussion upon which the conclusions are based.

Morally Relevant Variables in Cases of Influencing

Related to the influencer. *I* is either rational or irrational; that is, the person can or cannot be responsible for his or her actions. *I* influences others either intentionally or unintentionally, is either aware or unaware of the *C*, and is either aware or unaware of *M*.

Related to the change. *C* is beneficial, harmful, or neither to *R* and is beneficial, harmful, or neither to others.

Related to the receiver. *R* is either rational or irrational; that is, *R* either can or cannot be responsible for his or her actions; is either aware or unaware of the *C*; is either aware or unaware of the *M*; either consents or does not consent to *C*; and either consents or does not consent to *M*.

Related to the means. *M* is beneficial, harmful or neither to *R* and is beneficial, harmful, or neither to others.

JUDGING THE MORALITY OF INFLUENCE

A. Considerations Pertaining to the Influencer (I)

1. Is *I* acting rationally in doing whatever it is that is influencing *R*?

The reason why this question is important is that the answer will help us to determine whether *I*'s behavior can be classified as in the moral realm or outside of it; that is, nonmoral. For example, if *I* happens to be an infant who influences his mother by crying or smiling, the influencing could not be considered moral or immoral. Infants do not have the capacity for rational action. They cannot be responsible for their behavior. Hence, their influence on others is nonmoral.

Consider another possibility. Suppose I is a woman of reasonable intelligence, but happens to be in a situation of extreme duress (e.g., a gunman is threatening her life). Suppose further that in the response to the situation, she does something that influences others (e.g., screams and starts a general panic in a bank). One may well determine that a reasonable response in that situation is too much to expect; that I is not responsible for what she does, and her influence on others is nonmoral.

It could be assumed that the infant example is irrelevant for assessing the morality of the actions of counselors. One could not acquire a position in counseling without considerable capacity for rational action. However, situations of extreme duress can and do occur occasionally in counseling. Clients sometimes act in impulsive, unpredictable, even life-threatening ways. It may be unreasonable to expect a counselor to respond rationally regardless of the situation.

2. Is I influencing R intentionally or unintentionally?

Determining the intentions of I is important because people generally judge whether another person is acting morally or not on the basis of his or her intentions. If one is trying to benefit others, the actions are generally judged to be moral; if one is trying to harm others, the actions are generally judged immoral. This seems to hold true whether or not I's actions bring the intended results. For example, suppose a counselor is enamored of his attractive female client and attempts to seduce her, and that his only intention is to satisfy his sexual urge. Suppose that his efforts trigger a response of spontaneous rage in his client, and this emotional release happens to be exactly what she needs to make progress toward psychological recovery. If the counselor's intentions were known, it is likely that his or her actions would be judged immoral in spite of their beneficial results.

It must also be recognized that the efforts of counselors with the best of intentions do not always achieve beneficial results and may sometimes result in net harm to their clients. Human interactions are extremely complex. When people take actions with regard to others, it is often quite difficult to predict how they will respond. Omniscience is too much to expect of counselors, and reasonably selected strategies for helping clients can fail. Unsuccessful efforts are not necessarily immoral. Of course, if a counselor persists in a course of action when there is available evidence that the results are harmful, one is likely to question the moral justification of the counselor's actions regardless of his or her good intentions.

So far, I have maintained that the morality of I's actions is generally judged on the basis of I's intentions, but have only considered cases in which I has acted with some definite intention regarding R. It is also necessary to consider the morality of unintentional influencing.

If *I* is bribing *R*, or cajoling or persuading him or her to do something, it is probably true that *I*'s actions are intentional. However, it is clear that people's actions often influence others even when they have no intention of doing so. My lavish praise of a movie, or reports of mechanical problems with a particular make of automobile, may influence friends to see the movie or select a different kind of car even though I had no intention of influencing them in these ways. To hold people morally responsible for all of their unintended influences on others would be unreasonable. It is possible for even the most mundane and innocent of a person's actions to have effects not known to him or her on other people who are also not known. It would be equally unreasonable, however, to limit an individual's moral responsibility to the effects of his or her intended actions. Certainly, people are responsible for some of their influences in spite of the fact that they did not intend the results that actually occurred.

Sometimes good intentions relieve one of moral culpability, but sometimes they do not. Counselors often work with vulnerable people and should be aware that almost anything they do can significantly influence clients. For example, one would expect a rational-emotive therapist, using confrontation as a technique, to be alert to signs that the client is reaching the limit of tolerable stress. If damage results from his or her lack of attention to these signs, the statement, "I meant no harm" is not very convincing.

The counseling relationship suggests another important consideration. Certain roles like teaching and counseling seem to carry with them the obligation to influence clients in fairly specific ways. For example, teaching English composition seems to carry with it the responsibility to help students write better paragraphs. The role of counselor seems to carry with it the responsibility to help a client achieve better awareness, improved problem solving skills, or whatever the appropriate goal may be. Clearly, one cannot expect counselors to achieve a 100% success rate with their clients, but one can expect their work to meet certain standards and their intentions to be to help clients to the best of their ability.

3. Is *I* aware of the specific effects on *R* that his or her words and actions are contributing to?

Much of the discussion in No. 2 is also relevant here. In general, people seem to hold other individuals accountable for the influences they have on others that they are aware of, or can reasonably be expected to be aware of. For example, if I studiously watch Jack Nicklaus hit a golf ball and do my best to duplicate his swing, I can reasonably claim that Mr. Nicklaus has influenced my swing. However, if my efforts are unsuccessful, I cannot reasonably claim that he ruined my golf game. There are some situations in which one is morally responsible for influences he or she is unaware of. Sometimes *I*'s failure to recognize the influence he or she is having on *R* is a case of apathy, neglect, or carelessness.

About some cases of influencing others unknowingly, it is reasonable to observe, "He or she should have known better." Of course, determining which of a person's influences on others one can expect him or her to be aware of can be a difficult judgment.

The foregoing discussion suggests that morality and knowledge are closely related. The more one understands about the effects of his or her actions on others, the greater the capacity for both moral and immoral influencing. This observation might lead a muddled thinker to conclude that the best way to avoid influencing others immorally would be to remain as ignorant as possible about the effects of his or her actions on others. Of course, anyone who takes moral responsibility seriously tends to move in the opposite direction. Rather than closing his or her eyes to (or washing his or her hands of) what he or she does to others, the person would want to know as much as possible about the interests of others and the effects of his or her actions on them.

4. Is I aware of M; that is, what he or she is doing that is actually influencing R?

The importance of this question stems from the following two assumptions: (a) that some means of influencing are moral, and some are immoral (This will be discussed later.) and (b) that generally, one is responsible for influencing that is known to him or her and not responsible for influencing done unknowingly (This was discussed in the previous section.). Question 4 is important because there can be situations in which an influencer is aware that he or she is influencing another person, is also aware of the particular changes he hopes to induce in the other person, but remains unaware of the specific way in which he or she is influencing; that is, unaware of the actual M that influences R. Consider the following cases:

- During a session with a client, a counselor tries to restrict his own role to that of a sounding board. As the client talks about her situation and her problems, he carefully avoids influencing her toward any particular course of action. However, in spite of his intention, he may have influenced her significantly. He may have done so by responding to certain of her utterances but not to others. He may have posed questions in a way that made one of the client's options look much more or less desirable than others. It may have been something as subtle as the changes in his facial expressions as he listened to his client.
- A school counselor has called a bright senior to her office. He has decided to drop his chemistry class, and she wants to be sure that he understands the implications of his decision. After the session, the student decides to remain in the class. The counselor sincerely believes that the only means she used to change the boy's mind was honest forthright discussion of the implications of his decision. Her assessment

may be inaccurate. Someone else observing the session might describe what she did as cajolery, guilt manipulation, or intimidation.

In the first case, I is actually trying to avoid influencing R. In the second case, I is trying to influence R in one way but may actually be influencing R in another way. Let us consider to what extent it is reasonable to hold people morally responsible for Ms they are unaware they are using. Much discussed previously is relevant here. In informal social exchanges, people generally do not hold other people accountable for unknown and unintentional influencing. One expects counselors, as professionals, to be alert about their effects on clients. Nevertheless, counselors, like other human beings, may make errors in assessing the ways they are influencing their clients. One cannot expect omniscience; however, the unique nature of the counselor-client relationship and the potential for harm to the client make it important for counselors to take extra steps to recognize their own biases and to assess accurately how they are affecting their clients. Consultations with colleagues seem to be a good way to work on these tasks.

B. *Considerations Pertaining to the Receiver of Influence (R)*

1. Is R rational or irrational during the time he or she is being influenced by I?

This question is important because the morality of the way in which I is influencing R may depend on the extent to which R is capable of making reasonable decisions about his or her own life. Although a full explication of the concept of freedom is inappropriate here, it can be assumed that being free means, among other things, being able to make one's own deliberations about what to believe or what course of action to follow without undue interference from others. It seems safe to assume that most counselors recognize concern for the freedom of their clients as a moral obligation. Of course, the principle is abstract. It does not establish any specific courses of action for counselors. Much deliberation may be necessary to make judgments about how it applies to a given case, and reasonable persons may come to different conclusions about the morally correct course of action for the counselor.

Concern for the freedom of clients obliges counselors to make constant judgments about the capacities and dispositions of their clients to engage in rational deliberation and decision making. These judgments are necessary to help counselors decide how much and what kinds of influences on their clients are morally justified. If R is a small child, a psychotic, or a clearly senile person, it would be irresponsible for the counselor, in the name of freedom, to accept and support whatever decisions the client makes. On the other hand, if R is a mentally alert, fully functioning adult, it would be arrogant of the counselor to decide that he or she alone knows what is best for the client—that there is no need to waste time considering the client's perspective.

Persons seeking counseling are often somewhere in the middle between fully functioning and incapacitated, however, and it may be quite unclear to the counselor just how much and what kinds of responsibility clients are capable of assuming. Perhaps the most difficult kind of case occurs when an ostensibly reasonable client indicates an intention to do something that the counselor has good reason to believe will bring unnecessarily harmful consequences to the client or to others. Suppose that the counselor does his or her best to help the client become aware of the undesirable implications of the decision, but the client remains steadfast. If the harm that the counselor anticipates is relatively minor, he or she may be able to let it go, reasoning that the client may learn better by experience. But if the harm is serious, the counselor may have to consider a variety of more intrusive forms of influencing than the one noted above.

Determining how much and what forms of influencing are morally justified can be an extremely difficult judgment. The counselor, like all persons, has an obligation to take reasonable action to prevent harm, but he or she also has an obligation to recognize clients as free agents to the extent possible. At the same time, the counselor must be on guard against the paternalistic tendency to believe that disagreeing with a counselor is a clear indication that a client is not yet ready to make his or her own decisions about how to deal with the problems.

2. Is R aware of, and does he or she approve of C?
3. Is R aware of, and does he or she approve of M?

These questions are suggested by the commonly accepted principle of informed consent. They are based on the assumption that affecting a change, or trying to affect a change, in another person can be a serious moral matter. The principle of freedom discussed earlier would seem to obligate an I, at least prima facie, to make sure that R understands and approves of both the C that I will try to induce and the Ms that he or she will use. However, there can be many factors to consider in counseling situations that affect that obligation, such as the following:

- R may lack the mental or psychological competence required for informed consent. If R happens to be a young child, a psychotic, or incompetent in some other way, it may be simply impossible for him or her to understand the Cs and Ms and their implications. When this situation occurs, it seems clear that the counselor has an obligation to seek informed consent from guardians.

- In some situations R's awareness of and consent to C and M can be reasonably assumed. If R invites an insurance salesman to call on him or her, or if R is a college student who enrolls in a particular course, some degree of informed consent can be assumed. There are some conventional expectations regarding what insurance salesmen and college instructors will do. It cannot be assumed in either case, however, that R completely understands what I will be doing and gives consent to any M that I may select.

- The situation seems to be similar in counseling. When a person picks out a particular kind of counselor to help him or her deal with a problem, there are some reasonable expectations about what the counselor will do. But counselors, even less than teachers and insurance salesmen, can assume that their clients understand and give consent to the Cs and Ms they are offering. For one thing, the Cs and Ms are likely to be more esoteric than in the teaching and salesmanship situations. They are also likely to involve intimate aspects of the client's personality. The informed consent principle seems to suggest that a counseling client has every right to expect a full disclosure of the Cs that the counselor expects to occur in the client and the particular Ms that the counselor intends to use.

- However, there are some complexities in the application of the informed consent principle to counseling situations. Certainly, there are some counseling situations in which the Cs and Ms can be clearly established at the outset for the client to consider and accept or reject. For example, a behaviorist counselor and his client might agree that agoraphobia is the problem to be addressed and also agree that certain behavioral changes are the appropriate Cs. The counselor may describe the series of treatments he believes are needed to help the client overcome the problem and get the client's approval. There seems to be little difficulty in applying the informed consent principle to a case like this, but many counseling situations are quite unlike this one.

- There are enormous variations in the problems clients bring to counseling, in the goals that counselors pursue with their clients and in the techniques counselors select. A client may be too distressed or too confused to understand and make rational decisions about the Ms a counselor intends to use. It may take some time and much effort on the part of both counselor and client to clearly identify the client's problems and to establish counseling goals. It is difficult to see how the informed consent principle can be applied when the Cs are unknown.

- There may be situations in counseling in which there are good clinical reasons *not* to fully disclose to the client the specific Cs the counselor is trying to induce and the specific Ms he or she is using. For example, a marriage and family counselor may use a paradoxical procedure to provoke a therapeutically desirable revolt in a family member. If the counselor fully discloses what his or her strategy is and what effects on the client he or she hopes will occur, there may be no chance for the strategy to be successful. In many cases, these minor deceptions may be justified, but counselors who use them should recognize that they are taking it upon themselves, in these situations, to decide what is in the best interest of their clients and are responsible for the results.

- In some cases, it may be morally justified for counselors to influence their clients toward Cs and to use Ms even when the client has expressly withheld his or her consent. Of course, doing something in direct opposition to the will of the client is an extremely serious matter with legal as well as moral implications. Nonetheless, situations do occur in which counselors are compelled to consider extraordinary measures (e.g., a client clearly indicates his or her intention to commit suicide or to inflict serious harm on another person). The counselor may feel obliged to intervene. A counselor is totally convinced that his alcoholic or drug abusing client desperately needs a treatment program, but the client refuses to enroll in one: The counselor considers using questionable techniques (e.g., deceit, threats, bullying) to get the client in a program.

- A counselor who decides to influence a client toward Cs and/or to use Ms when the client disapproves, should recognize the gravity of the decision. That counselor is so sure that he or she is right about the assessment of what the client needs and so sure that the client is wrong, that he or she actively overrules the client's viewpoint. The counselor would need extremely good grounds to justify this apparent deprivation of the client's freedom.

C. Considerations Pertaining to the Changes (Cs)

1. Are the Cs toward which the counselor is influencing the client beneficial, harmful, or neither?
2. Are the Cs beneficial, harmful, or neither to others?

When applied to the preponderance of counseling cases, the answer to Question 1 seems quite simple. The changes brought about by counseling are usually changes that clients desire and changes that reasonable people would agree are good for clients. Some typical counseling Cs that seem to fit this description are the following:

- Increasing self-reliance and initiative
- Increasing social sensitivity

- Improving communication between marriage partners
- Finding a suitable occupation
- Overcoming alcoholism or a drug addiction

In most cases there is probably little doubt about the worth of the Cs toward which counselors direct their efforts. Of course, there is the occasional case in which a counselor works to prevent a desirable change or to change a client in an undesirable way (e.g., keeping a client dependent to maintain income). But it should be assumed that the vast majority of counselors do their best to help clients alter their lives in ways that are beneficial.

There can be many kinds of cases, however, in which even a completely conscientious counselor has difficulty determining whether a C would be desirable. Sometimes the problem is the difficulty of assessing the consequences of a C. Should this teenager have an abortion? Should this marriage be saved? Should this client make a career change? It is possible for a C to promise short-term relief but also involve longer term risk, or it could be the other way around: immediate discomfort, tension, or pain but the promise of a brighter future in the long run. Fortunately, in most cases it is the client and not the counselor who has to assume major responsibility for such serious decisions. The counselor does what he or she can to help the client make a decision in a calm and rational manner with full understanding of the implications. Of course, as we have discussed previously, the counselor cannot always assume that the client is capable of being responsible for serious decision making.

Another difficulty in assessing the desirability of a C stems from the fact that it is rarely the case that a C has important implications for only one person. A counselor who is working with a couple, a family, or another kind of group may come to the realization that a given C would be beneficial for some members of the group but harmful to others. Even when a counselor is working with a single client, it seems irresponsible for him or her to ignore the possible effects of the client's decisions on significant others in the client's life. At the least, it seems to be the counselor's responsibility to make sure the client is aware of these implications. What the counselor should do in the case in which the client refuses to give serious consideration to the effects of decisions on others could be a very sticky moral problem.

D. Considerations Pertaining to the Means (Ms)

1. Are the Ms beneficial, harmful, or neither to the client?
2. Are the Ms beneficial, harmful, or neither to others?

Much of the discussion of C is also relevant in reference to M. Determining the benefits or harm of a given M can sometimes be a difficult task. An M that benefits one client may harm another. An M that is reasonable to use when working with an adult may not be suitable for use with children. An M can have immediate ill effects on a client, but promise long-term benefits, or it could be the other way around—immediate benefits, long-term harm.

These considerations are tough enough, but the counselor also needs to consider the relationships between Ms and Cs. This can lead to some complex means-ends problems: For example, does the great value of the C that the counselor and client have established as a goal justify the use of a particular M that is risky, painful, or has serious side effects? Fortunately, as was discussed earlier, there are many situations in which the major responsibility for decisions regarding the use of particular Ms is the client's. There is one important difference, however, when the decisions are about Ms rather than Cs. The counselor is in a much better position than the client to know what alternative Ms are available to deal with the client's problems and what are the likely effects of the use of those Ms. The principle of informed consent suggests that the counselor has an obligation to give the client a full and impartial explanation of available options, avoiding the temptation of skewing the discussion toward the Ms that are simply the personal favorites of the counselor.

In some cases, as was discussed earlier, the counselor may have good reason for the use of an M without the prior informed consent of a client (e.g., when using a paradoxical procedure). In such cases, the counselor assumes full responsibility for the results. No doubt, there are situations in which the use of covert methods by counselors is justified, but it seems wise for a counselor to move with considerable caution in this area. It may be true that the success of an M may require the client to be unaware of it. He or she is thus deprived of the opportunity to consider the M and decide whether it is desirable. If the counselor keeps his or her Ms *very* secret, everyone else is also deprived of this opportunity. It seems desirable for a counselor to submit his or her covert Ms to the scrutiny of other counselors. Colleagues may see implications that the counselor is unaware of.

There are some cases in which the Ms selected are clearly immoral simply because they are inhumane, for example, the use of cattle prods, electric shock treatments, or medication just to make custodial care easier, ignoring the effects of the treatment on the patient or client. But there are also cases in which determining the justification of various Ms is a much more difficult problem than this. Perhaps the most difficult judgment regarding Ms that a counselor must make is determining how much intrusion into the client's deliberating and choice-making processes is morally justified by the client's present condition. If the client is incapable of rational deliberation, someone else will have to determine whether or not the counselor's choice of Ms is reasonable and appropriate. If the client is mature and fully rational, the counselor can talk over various alternative Ms with the client and get informed consent. Perhaps the most difficult situation occurs when a client's mental or psychological condition is somewhere in the middle; not so bad that others must assume responsibility for his or her welfare, but not so good that the person can assume full responsibility for his or her decisions. People seek counseling for many reasons. Quite often it is because they are having trouble seeing their situation clearly and determining what course of action has the best chance for improving their lives. Sometimes it is a problem that they recognize but cannot overcome without help. They are vulnerable and, to some extent, dependent on the counselor to make things better.

The relatively vulnerable state of the client adds to the moral responsibility of the counselor. He or she may be in a position to be a powerful influence in the client's life. The client may simply want the counselor to get rid of the trouble, with little concern about the freedom to make his or her own deliberations and choices. The fact that the client lacks concern about freedom, however, does not seem to justify the counselor not having concern about it. The counselor who is seriously committed to respecting the client's freedom must make many judgments concerning which decisions the client is ready to be responsible for.

The recognition that a client is in a vulnerable condition raises moral questions about the use of some *M*s that may not arise in other influencing situations. In many contexts outside of counseling, one person helps another to deliberate about a problem and come to a decision without having to worry about too much intrusion on the other person's freedom. People give each other information, opinions about a situation, suggestions, and advice with the assumption that the *R* will sift through their contributions and decide for himself or herself which of the ideas to use and which to reject. A perplexed and vulnerable client, however, may interpret a counselor's opinions as pronouncements of truth and a counselor's advice as commands that cannot be rejected. With a vulnerable client, an unwary counselor may be more influential than he or she intended. More important, he or she may be more influential than is morally justified.

Of course, there are some *M*s that raise moral questions in any context in which they are used. If an *I* stacks an argument, flatters, makes an appeal to love or to friendship, or engages in guilt manipulation, it is quite likely that he or she is interfering with the *R*s attempt to deliberate in a rational matter. If an *I* bribes or threatens an *R*, he or she is probably jeopardizing the *R*s chances of making a free choice. It is hard to imagine a situation in counseling that would justify the use of any of these *M*s.

CONCLUSION

In this analysis I have formulated a matrix of influence and have used the matrix to identify the factors that must be taken into consideration in analyzing the morality of various acts of influencing. I found that many counseling situations are too complex for this study to establish specific moral obligations for counselors. Much depends on the combination of factors in

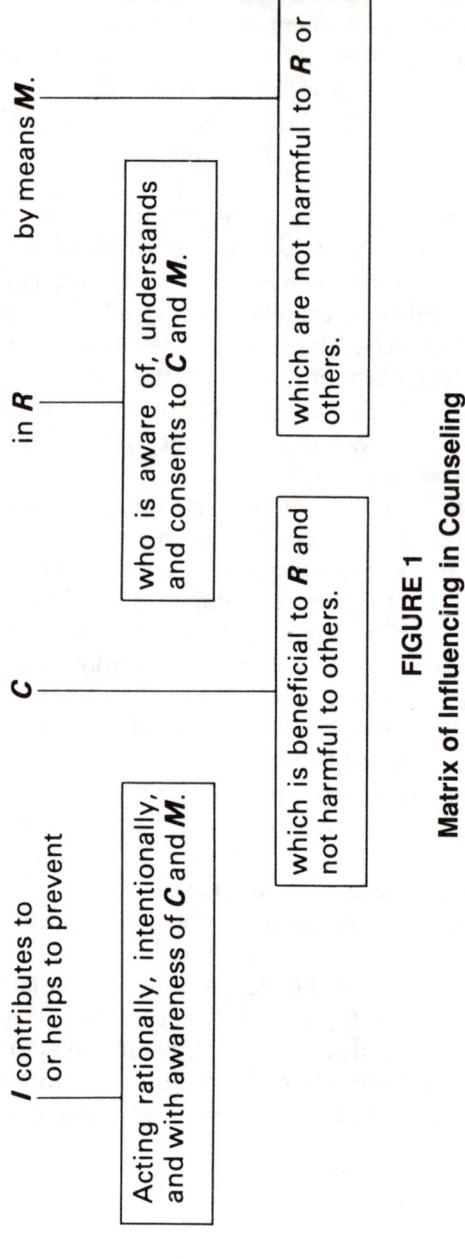

FIGURE 1
Matrix of Influencing in Counseling

a given case. But my analysis seems to suggest some broad requirements for acts of influencing to be moral. If all of the moral considerations discussed in this study are added to the matrix (see Figure 1), it is possible to derive a description of acts of influencing, the morality of which seems beyond question.

There are probably few cases of influencing in counseling or other contexts that meet all the requirements of this description. That does *not* mean that there is immorality involved in almost all cases of influencing. It does mean that in regard to most cases of influencing, there are moral questions to be addressed. It seems especially important for counselors to address the moral questions pertaining to their influence on clients.

REFERENCES

Baier, L. (1965). *The moral point of view*. New York: Random House.

Bergin, A. E. (1985). Proposed values for guiding and evaluating counseling and psychotherapy. *Counseling and Values, 29*, 99–116.

Breggin, P. (1971). Psychotherapy as applied ethics. *Psychiatry, 34*, 59–74.

Brody, B. (Ed.). (1970). *Moral rules and particular circumstances*. Englewood Cliffs, NJ: Prentice-Hall.

Carroll, M., Schneider, H., & Wesley, G. (1985). *Ethics in the practice of psychology* (Chapter 1). Englewood Cliffs, NJ: Prentice-Hall.

Downie, R., & Telfer, E. (1969). *Respect for persons*. London, England: George Allen and Unwin.

Edward, R. (1982). *Psychiatry and ethics*. New York: Prometheus Books.

Fried, C. (1970). *An anatomy of values*. London, England: Oxford University Press.

Gert, B. (1973). *The moral rules*. New York: Harper & Row.

Karasu, T. (1980). The ethics of psychotherapy. *The American Journal of Psychiatry, 137*, 1502–1512.

London, P. (1964). *Modes and morals of psychotherapy*. New York: Holt, Rinehart and Winston.

Lowe, C. (1976). *Value orientations in counseling*. Cranston, RI: Carroll Press.

Macklin, R. (1973). Values in psychoanalysis and psychotherapy: A survey and analysis. *American Journal of Psychoanalysis, 33*, 133–150.

MacLagan, W., (1960). Respect for persons as a moral principle, I and II. *Philosophy, 35*, 193–217, 289–305.

Peters, R. (1974). *Psychology and ethical development* (Chapter 14). London, England: George Allen and Unwin.

Peterson, J. (1976). *Counseling and values: A philosophical examination*. Cranston, RI: Carroll Press.

Rosenbaum, M. (1982). *Ethics and values in psychotherapy*. New York: Free Press.

Guilt

DAVID BELGUM

THE ARCHETYPE OF a guilty person was King David, who arranged to have gorgeous Bathsheba's husband killed so he could satisfy his desire, which first grew within him upon seeing her bathing.

> "Wash me thoroughly from my iniquity,
> and cleanse me from my sin
> For I acknowledge my transgression:
> and my sin is ever before me.
> Against thee, thee only, have I sinned,
> and done this evil in thy sight . . ." (Psalm 51:2–4a)

This is not a case of "guilt feelings," nor does the King provide any rationalization or mitigating circumstances. In the Hebrew Bible guilt was clearcut and straightforward.

We may look up to so great a saint as Paul, yet guilt was there, too, in abundance:

> So I find it to be a law that when I want to do right, evil lies close at hand. For I delight in the law of God, in my inmost self, but I see in my members another law at war with the law of my mind and making me captive to the law of sin which dwells in my members. Wretched man that I am! Who will deliver me from this body of death? (*Romans* 7:21–24)

From the classic Roman period we have derived a term that survived in the Roman Catholic confessional—"culpa." ("It is my fault, my grievous fault, my most grievous fault.") It means more than a mistake. "We all feel the responsibility for the wrong deed, attached to "culpa" (Wilhelm-Hooijbergh, 1954, p. 38). For all our stereotyping of ancient Rome as wanton and decadent, they still had a clear concept of sin and guilt.

For the purpose of this article we will assume that guilt pertains to one's thoughts, words, or deeds, whereas shame refers to one's nature (i.e., "It's a shame he's so short"). One may be ashamed of simply having a cleft palate or club foot without having done anything to "earn" the rejection or disapproval of parents or peers. It is not appropriate to expect a person to repent of being shorter than his basketball coach father would have liked or to make restitution for her cleft palate. In Eriksonian terms of stigma of shame implies it is not all right to *be* who you *are*; whereas guilt points to the fact that it was not all right to *do* what you *did*. What they both have in common is loss of self-esteem, but because of their different dynamics and meaning they need to be treated quite differently. The one afflicted with shame needs to accept what may not be changeable (e.g., shortness,). The guilty party needs to change in some tangible ways such as making restitution and amending behavior, seeking reconciliation through repentance, and confession.

Eberhard (1967) begins his book about sin and guilt in China with a discussion of the old controversy whether some cultures are more shame oriented, whereas others rely on guilt for social control. "Loss of face" is very significant in the Orient. Eberhard says of the traditional period "that the Chinese did not believe in a blind fate, that the individual was responsible for his fate, and that his actions, even though they may remain unknown to society, are known to the deities and receive punishment (or reward)" (pp. 14–15).

From contemporary China we have also witnessed how guilt is dependent on society's norms at a given time. What was considered a virtue under Confucian standards was cause for guilt under Mao's Cultural Revolution; then, after the arrest of the Gang of Four, persons who previously had been considered guilty and worthy of imprisonment, were later rehabilitated and declared once again to be in a state of grace.

I shall make no effort to define guilt in an ontological sense because we live in a pluralistic world, and because the content of guilt is functionally defined by our own particular culture group. Thus, even though the substance of guilt may vary from one age or ethnic group to another, the dynamic of guilt is universal. At any given time and place there are behaviors believed to be desired, positive, constructive, and useful for society and others behaviors that are seen and experienced as undesirable, destructive, and counterproductive for society as well as for the individual.

THE DYNAMIC FUNCTION OF MORALITY AND GUILT

Guilt is multifaceted: Moral evil as an injury by a person to the self is *vice*; moral evil as an offense by a person against human society is *crime*; moral evil as a person affecting one's relation to God in *sin*. Often all three facets are involved (e.g., when one damages one's own reputation by the disgrace of theft, has offended the shopkeeper, and violated one of the Ten Commandments all at the same time). One may also be guilty of a breach of etiquette (and may pay heavily for it) even though it is not included in any divine proscription; furthermore, a person may covet another's spouse in such a way that it is unknown to anyone else in society (yet clearly forbidden in one of the Commandments).

Some religious interpretations present mortality in negative terms. Even the wording of the Ten Commandments ("thou shalt not") contributes to this attitude. God looked down on his people and saw they were having too much fun, so he decided to curtail their activities: limit them to their own spouses, confine them to milking their own goats, and stop worshipping things that were not ultimate (e.g., carousing around a golden calf). In popular parlance this is stated as "Anything that is any fun is either fattening or immoral."

Persons who have such a negative view of moral guidelines will resent something as simple as traffic lights. They will curse the red light that makes them late for work, but they will not appreciate the last three green lights that allowed them to pass through busy intersections safely without waiting.

From a larger perspective the ordering of society can be viewed as the useful alternative to chaos. Individuals may feel more secure when there is a consensus about basic value issues involving their person, their interpersonal relationships, their property, and their rights and obligations.

Although in our contemporary American society we have just come out of a period of denial of death, we are still ambivalent, confused, and hung up on a denial of guilt. The usefulness of morality is diminished when it is not spoken of with one voice. Most tribes were marked by a consensus about moral questions and standards; but our youth grow up in a society where there may well be five standards concerning a matter within one city block. Where morality is concerned, The United States is not a melting pot but rather a tossed salad. Some values are in a drastic state of revision (Amato, 1982). Religion cannot be counted on to provide the same kind of support for morality today as in the past because its influence seems to have diminished drastically (Knight, 1969). In addition to the question of which criteria are ideal, we need to ask the question of what function morality fulfills in social interaction and in personality.

The Usefulness of Constructive Morality and Realistic Guilt

When we belong to a group, it is assumed that we have certain obligations to (literally meaning "bound to") the group. When we commit offenses or violate the group's standards, we are met with ill will and anger on the part of others. Guilt is the anger turned toward ourselves, corresponding to the anger we would feel toward anyone else doing the same thing. This is simply a natural and necessary reaction; without it morality would be meaningless. It is patently contradictory to say "It is very important to respect another's property; but it doesn't really matter if you steal it." Just as two objects cannot occupy the same space in physics, a behavior cannot be helpfully described as good and bad at the same time in ethics (except by a person committed to situation ethics). The complex discipline of ethics is the effort to arrive systematically and objectively at a decision whether a behavior is or is not morally defensible.

Fortunately, the dynamic of morality works pretty well most of the time, and we can find our tools, car, and other property where we left them; others do not bear much false witness about us; and our contracts are almost always honored by banks and businesses. We often take this working of moral principles for granted and are not even conscious of our ethical decisions. If we have been well socialized, we do not have to decide whether to steal something every time we enter a store.

Guilt in the moral sphere is analogous to pain in the bodily context. Physical pain alerts the person to some maladjustment, disease, pressure, injury, or malalignment (lower back pain). This provides the person with the opportunity to do something about the pain: remove the splinter, place splints on either side of the broken arm, or become available for slipped disc surgery. A woman in Canada was reported as having the unfortunate problem of not being able to experience pain; hence she was in great danger because she could have a rusty nail grinding away at her foot without knowing about it, with the potential for blood poisoning or other infection. She could burn her hand on the stove and not perceive of the need to remove it from the hot burner.

The sociopath has much the same problem in the psycho-social sphere, not worrying about the fact that this or that behavior is alienating others. Meanwhile, the sociopath may be feeling, "I never had any meaningful relationships anyway, so what is there to lose?" This is why O. Hobart Mowrer often told a counselee in his integrity therapy group, "Fortunately you had enough character to get sick over it." The assumption of his approach was that morality was a positive force and guilt a useful voice calling us back to responsibility to our group of "significant others" (Drakeford, 1967, Mowrer, 1961).

Wherever we look in social enterprises and groups we see reciprocity of social contract. In business transactions the buyer and seller each have responsibilities, violations of which can lead to small claims court. Football players must follow certain rules for the game to progress in an orderly fashion, and hockey players can end up in the "penalty box." Responsibility rests on each person to carry out his or her obligations whether it be in the role of parent, citizen, student, neighbor, friend, employee or employer, or therapist or client.

Acting or speaking in a way that is destructive to the relationship or social contract results in loss of the benefits of that membership or role. Guilt is the negative emotion associated with that loss and the attendant alienation that accompanies it. As long as one wishes to be a member in good standing in some group, it is usually obligatory to pay one's dues, literally, what is due the group. Then one can also enjoy the benefits of group membership whether it be fellowship, protection, security, status, or even economic rewards. If a person violates this responsibility, the results are guilt and a painful awareness of loneliness, which, if things are working constructively, could goad him or her into some action designed to restore the relationship, to bring about reconciliation, to regain one's place in the group, and to return to good standing. Then the pain of guilt will have served its purpose just as the pain of removing the splinter was "worth it" if it resulted in getting rid of the foreign object with its danger of infection.

When Guilt Is Distorted and Nonfunctional

In defining objective, realistic guilt, we mean the violation of the standard of behavior and attitude that is considered acceptable for membership in good standing in one's group of significant others. These standards for acceptance can range from such generic expectations as respecting another's property (e.g., not stealing it) to paying one's annual club membership dues. They can be as general as patriotism toward one's country or loyalty toward one's political party and as specific as observing the policy and procedure manual of one's company or the institution for which one works. The degree of seriousness with which the guilt is viewed by one's group varies with the consequences of the offense. Treason in wartime could lead to death, whereas violating an institutional procedure might draw only a supervisor's rebuke in private conference.

Distorted, nonfunctional, or neurotic guilt describes how one feels about a *presumed* violation about which there really is no such consensus in the group to which one belongs. Everyone in the group approves of the person's commitment and efforts on behalf of the group, yet this "guilty" one feels he or she has not "done enough." He or she is operating under some private moral system or using his or her self-evaluation in a symbolic manner, perhaps trying to win approval indirectly or atone for some previous unworthiness; it is not objectively related to the current standards of his or her group concerning the presumed "violation."

Inappropriate guilt does not lead to constructive personality functioning. The perfectionist misuses morality, complains about getting 98% on an exam when 100% was so close at hand. We get some notion of the origin of this scrupulosity when the student further complains, "What will my Dad say when I bring this exam home?" The workaholic feels guilty about not satisfactorily doing the work of two, which turns out not to be very helpful for one's successor. One such minister, lacking a balanced perspective, was helped to see that while he was in a desperate pursuit for righteousness in his dedicated service, he was actually violating the commandment about taking one day off out of every seven for rest and refreshment. He had the arrogance to think that although his parishioners needed a sabbath, he was different. Once he reorientated his values, he could quit feeling guilty about doing right, namely, fulfilling his role within a reasonable job description.

The above instances do not involve "real," objective guilt, but rather a distortion. It is a case of distorted ethical thinking. One of the diagnostic tasks of a priest in the confessional situation is to sort out scrupulosity and neurotic guilt from legitimate, or, what we have called "real" guilt. A person may simply be misinformed about what her or his religious denomination or ethnic group requires in a given circumstance and hence he or she may feel unnecessarily guilty about something that is perfectly acceptable. The person who has stolen $100 should feel guilty. The newlywed couple who decided to rent their own apartment instead of accepting the generous offer of the parents to continue living at the bride's childhood home need not feel guilty about their decision. We should not dismiss so-called neurotic guilt too quickly because it may only be indicator of a larger problem. Such was the case of the patient at Moose Lake State Hospital who had a hand-washing compulsion. He washed and rubbed his hands even though they were not dirty, but it was still true that his hands had done something dirty; he had sexually molested a little neighbor girl. As often as not, seemingly inappropriate guilt expressions for trivial matters may indeed point in the direction of a values problem; otherwise why did the client select value language?

Within some families we see guilt used as a motivational force. Gunn (1978) cautions against being manipulated by guilt. Deathbed promises can fall into this category (e.g, "Promise me you'll never sell the farm"). An elderly parent can hope to extract favors from a son or daughter by reminding the person that "As alcoholic as your father was, I stayed married for the sake of you children." "If you loved me you would do _____ ." One needs to speak up responsibly to others who try to make one feel guilty inappropriately. We need clear criteria as to the limits of our responsibility so as not to be caught in the web of impossible and misplaced obligations. Little children cannot be expected to set these limits on their own; the process of maturation brings with it the final adult task of deciding on our own what are legitimate and reasonable standards. We each need to find that healthy balance of moral life that avoids either extreme of perfectionism or sociopathy. Each decade or generation has it own temptations to distortion whether it be the rigid victorianism of the past or the laissez-faire permissiveness that some espouse today.

Some counselees have become immobilized, or have damaged others, by the very values that were intended to facilitate constructive action and guidance, good relationships, and peace of mind. They have distorted or exaggerated some very fine ideals such as love, service, dedication, and patriotism. A parent, fearful of not being "good enough," may so smother the child with love and protection that he or she becomes hopelessly dependent and fixated in a child-like stage. Albert Ellis' Rational-Emotive Therapy can help some clients see the distortions in their own approach to morality and the irrational ideas that have been guiding them. Psychiatrists and theologians alike have pointed out the problems involved with distorted and neurotic guilt (Bier, 1971; Knight, 1969; McKenzie, 1962).

Levels of Responsibility

The concept of "diminished responsibility," "not guilty by reason of insanity," and "irresistible impulse," can be traced back at least to the famous M'Naghten Case in England. In quaint leglese it went something like this:

Daniel M'Naghten, a certain pistol (in his hand) of the value of 20s, loaded and charged with gunpowder and a leaden bullet . . . of his malice aforethought did strike, penetrate, and wound . . . kill and murder the said Edward Drummond. The prisoner pleaded Not Guilty. (Clark & Finnelly, 1901, p. 719)

Although it was true he was suffering from delusions and was admittedly mentally unstable, the public was incensed because M'Naghten had intended to kill Prime Minister Peel and had mistaken his secretary, Drummond, for him. Here was the smoking gun, and he had the audacity to plead "Not Guilty." The Parliament asked the judges of the high court to come up with some policy statement that could cover cases like this in the future. Hence, the M'Naghten Rule, which reads in part that

to establish a defense of insanity, it must be clearly proved that, at the time of committing the act, the party accused was laboring under such a defect of reason, from disease of mind, as not to know the nature and quality of the act he was doing was wrong; or if he did know it, that he did not know he was doing what was wrong." (*Encyclopaedia Britannica*, 1978, pp. 367–368)

The relationship of guilt to responsibility is a complex problem (Clyne, 1973; Ross, 1975).

Another great milestone in the development of diminished responsibility was Freud's interpretation of the unconscious. Thoughts, wishes, and motives that lie hidden in the unconscious are beyond our willful control. He saw psychopathology in everyday life, in slips of the tongue, in unintentional forgetting, and in humor. Perhaps the difference between normal persons and the mentally ill is a matter of degree, or the fact that certain of our defense mechanisms simply fit well into our environment (such as the compulsive accountant). An artist may be unmindful of why his or her favorite colors are yellows and browns until analysis finally links them up with premature and difficult toilet training. The same goes for those who need to rebel against authority even though the father is long dead. If all this were true, it is doubtful whether one could speak about responsibility for moral decisions and behavior or about guilt in the commonly understood sense of the term. Although Freud saw the necessity for social order, he assumed that the price we would have to pay for the civilizing effects of morality would be neurosis (Freud, 1961).

Finally, the mechanisms of determinism were demonstrated by Watson, and later Skinner, in such a convincing and scientifically controlled manner that it seemed there was less and less of our behavior that we shaped or decided for ourselves. We were largely the result of our conditionings. Finally when comedian Flip Wilson said in his impish way, "The Devil made me do it," it seemed as though we had come full circle. Primitive society believed we were conditioned by good and evil spirits; modern scientific psychology proved we were conditioned by outside forces and past shapings by parents and social influence. How could one be held responsible in any meaningful sense? Yet in the everyday affairs of the public forum and market place, persons continue to be held responsible for traffic tickets and mortgage payments. No wonder people are confused about moral responsibility and guilt.

An Alternate View

No one need deny the limits that both nature and nurture place on our freedom, but it seems useful to maximize our capacity for self-determination and responsibility. We can realize our potential by striving to be as responsible as possible rather than searching for rationalizations to minimize and limit the sphere of our responsibility.

Let us reconsider the moral significance of the unconscious. Perhaps we have had more options than we acknowledge. True, when an unresolved conflict becomes repressed into the subconscious, we have placed it beyond willful control, but who did the repressing if not ourselves? Certainly not our neighbor. It may have seemed the easier way out—to deny the anger rather than deal with it in a straightforward manner. Even that choice to repress is one we would do well to claim responsibility for; successful therapy helps the person to own up to that choice and to try to make a more realistic and workable choice the next time. A large part of the problem has been one of value choice. A holistic view of personality implies that the whole of the person belongs to the person and not someone else; the unconscious as well as the conscious is part of our personhood and does not belong to someone else no matter how much he or she may have tampered with it or tried to claim ownership and proprietorship over it. Martyrs have understood this clearly when they have said, "Do with me what you will; I am still in my own person."

The person who has his or her own integrity does not seek eagerly for rationalizations or mitigating circumstances to avoid responsibility. We need not be judgmental and harsh toward persons who use defense mechanisms such as projection to avoid difficult confrontations or failures because none of us have always successfully dealt with our life's problems or failures; however, we can aim toward a more responsible method of problem solving.

A strong belief in determinism may seem to soften our blunders with "diminished responsibility," but what a person believes about the determinism-freedom issue goes a long way toward shaping one's response. The rehabilitation patient who waits passively for "others" (i.e., physician, physical therapist, or social worker) to provide the healing is a poor prospect for recovery. The client who invests self with a sense of responsibility, purpose, and mission in life is already headed in the right direction; the whole staff feels more optimistic about this person's rehabilitation. Likewise the counselee who believes deterministic conditioning has wrought the havoc is the one who sits back and hopes someone else will start conditioning and moulding a new personality and a new solution. The prospects are correspondingly bleak.

The level of responsibility accepted is crucial in psychotherapy and counseling; there is no way of avoiding the necessity of dealing with guilt along the way. What the counselor or therapist believes about the function of morality and guilt is also of significance and will have ramifications for both diagnosis and treatment.

DIAGNOSIS

One mental patient asked to see a chaplain to talk about a "moral matter." He was depressed and spoke about his "unworthiness." One assumption about depressed persons is that they are too hard on themselves. But we must listen objectively to the client's story and not come with preconceived notions to fit our own theory. This patient began to unfold an unsavory story of promiscuity, using women for his own purposes, and feeling intermittently guilty about his unfaithfulness to any one for any length of time. As he reported his opportunism and egocentrism, it became fairly clear that his self-diagnosis of being an "unworthy person" was accurate and reflected a touch of responsible realism. His attitude fit Mowrer's definition of guilt: if you have done something you do not want to have known (especially by significant others). No wonder he and many like him are especially interested in "confidentiality."

Another patient felt guilty for being the cause of her newborn baby's mongolism. She was sure God had punished her, quite fittingly and justly, for her premarital indiscretions. The geneticist, her obstetrician, and pediatrician had all given her scientific assurances that the baby's mongolism was not caused be her indiscretions. But the guilt remained. Neither the counselor nor anyone else needed to point out her problem; she diagnosed it herself. Her behavior had not really any causal effect on her baby; however, she did need to deal with moral indiscretions from the past for which she felt guilty. A quick reassurance would have short-circuited the process she needed to go through (i.e., a reconciliation, a dealing with past guilt, and returning to what her church called "a state of grace."

The "presenting symptom" or initially-stated guilty event may not be the key issue but only the first "trial balloon" that the counselee sends up to test the counselor. If the counselor cannot handle the test issue raised, the client is relieved not to have come out with the "really horrid" matter at the beginning. Judgmentalism prevents an accurate diagnosis especially when a matter of guilt is involved.

A woman, who labored under guilty feelings for hating her mother so much in spite of having been her faithful caretaker for 20 years, was helped to see that the hatred was only a secondary mistake. She had acted irresponsibly when she allowed her mother to dominate her, interfere with her marriage, and manipulate her for many years. This was accepting a basic responsibility and confessing a more basic sin from which the hatred was only a spin-off. She need not have fallen into this bondage but could have followed the mandate for adulthood of her own tradition quoted in marriage ceremonies: For this reason a person shall leave father and mother and be joined to one's spouse, and the two shall become one (paraphrase of *Matthew* 19:5–6a). Naturally, the counselor did not, and should not, point this out in didactic fashion but helped her discover it for herself as she reviewed the long and tumultuous journey she had had with her mother over the last 25 years. We need to distinguish the symptoms from the actual problem. It requires sensitivity and careful diagnosis to know when the core of the guilt problem has been reached.

The problem may not really be a matter of guilt, although that is what the client presents. A case in point is the student who felt guilty about not getting high grades like the two older siblings. A careful review of the student's admissions documents and test scores by the guidance counselor revealed that the student was actually quite average in capacity and aptitude, and "average grades" were entirely appropriate and a realistic evaluation of performance and potential. What was needed was acceptance of self, not forgiveness for failure and faults. The student was later able to use this new insight in settling on a more suitable and less ambitious vocational goal. Also relationships with the siblings became more relaxed and less competitive.

If a client is depressed or incapacitated by anxiety, there may be many reasons or causes (e.g., metabolism, brain damage, genetics, and child abuse). Medication, surgery, or counseling may be appropriate. We need to mend the garment where it is torn. If guilt is indicated as a result of careful diagnosis and self-disclosure on the part of the client, then we need to pursue an appropriate mode of treatment.

TREATMENT

How does the average citizen treat a confession of guilt on the part of another person? It seems most people deal with it awkwardly. In asking a variety of friends and acquaintances how they would deal with the following situation, a general pattern emerged. Let us say that a person drove 50 miles to have an appointment with you, but you completely forgot about it and had joined a foursome for golf. You are mortified and the next time you see the person you say, "I am so sorry I missed the appointment. It was very irresponsible of me; I apologize." What would the other person be most likely to reply? Most said something like the following: "Oh, that's OK." "Think nothing of it," "That's all right," "Forget it." Now actually, it was not "all right;" it was really a wrong thing to do. Why, then, the avoidance of its moral dimension or the trivializing of the matter? Perhaps to deal with it in a straightforward way (i.e., on a moral level, by saying, "I forgive you") sounds too self-righteous. There is an embarrassment about seeming to stand on higher ground and forgiving this inferior person who made the bad mistake. Perhaps all generations have wrestled with this, and it is not any more difficult now than in times past. Linguistic symbols change and new liturgies emerge, but the choice of terms is worth studying.

Punishment is a treatment that can take many forms. One is to leave the penitent in the sin by withholding forgiveness or reconciliation. The other person responds severely, "What good does that do to talk about it? What is done is done!" Garrison Keillor of radio fame has said that in Lake Wobegon, Minnesota, "Sins are not something to be forgiven, but to be treasured," because people do not let it drop, but rub it in periodically for years. Persons have met with unhelpful responses so often that they are fearful to make yet another confession.

In counseling it is assumed essential to meet the client on his or her own level of mood, content, and purpose. It is possible to meet the client on the moral level with compassion and grace. For this to be effective the counselor needs a wholesome attitude toward morality as a function and guilt as a powerful and often appropriate experience. If morality is seen as basically negative and moral discourse a cause for discomfort, then the counselor will not be available or helpful in working through the problem of guilt. Perhaps the counselor has never experienced constructive reconciliation, restitution, forgiveness, or grace. Then we have the blind leading the blind.

On the other hand, if the counselor has been grievously estranged from a significant other (family member, co-worker, or friend) and has become reconciled through confession and forgiveness then we have one beggar showing the other beggar where the food is. The conversation will be authentic; there will be no embarrassment about the moral level of discourse and no danger of conveying a sense of moral superiority. It is the kind of integrity and openness with which an Alcoholics Anonymous member relates to another alcoholic. This is the healing of the Balm of Gilead.

Today, with the stress on the "ministry of the laity," many counselees will gladly receive words of assurance, reconciliation and forgiveness from a lay counselor; however, there will be others who really need to go back to their faith group and receive absolution from their own priest, minister, or rabbi. In this case the counselor has been a facilitator and appropriate referring agent. There are many excellent relationships between a variety of counselors and local clergy, a useful interdisciplinary teamwork. When the primary focus is on helping the client meet urgent needs, professionals do not worry about territoriality or professional rivalry. It is helpful for counselors to acquaint themselves with local clergy with whom they can feel comfortable in a working partnership especially in the areas of values and guilt.

A serious gap in the therapy for guilt is the fact that often the counselor or clergy believe the problem is resolved once the catharsis of confession has happened or the absolution has been pronounced. A functional confessional (Belgum, 1963) is incomplete without the implementation of a new set of constructive behaviors to replace the destructive patterns that have recently been repented. The client needs to reinvest the new energy, released when the guilty burden has been laid down, into a new life style, restitution, or what the Catholics call "satisfaction" (i.e., living satisfactorily instead of guiltily). Moral theology holds that if a person is not "aversive" toward the sin that got him or her into trouble, the penitent was not authentically repentant, and the healing is incomplete. But the future will not take care of itself automatically. The client needs support, guidance, and a positive behavior modification for some period of time until new habits, new relationships, and the satisfaction of a new life will sustain the person so recently recovered. Support groups and encouragement are needed for positive reinforcement of the new patterns so that the classic repetition does not occur; when a demon was driven out of the house and it was swept and clean, seven other demons saw it was empty and reoccupied it; and the later state of that house was worse than the former (paraphrased from Luke 11:24–26).

SUMMARY

Once we are willing to be open to the possibility that guilt may be a part of our client's problem, new opportunities and directions open up for our work. But we need to be careful about our own attitude toward and use of morality and our own perception of the function of guilt. Then we need to assess and diagnose the moral dimension accurately, of course, with the help of the client's interpretation. Finally, if we feel uneasy about treating this problem, we have many willing and competent partners among the clergy if we are alert to seeking them out and making referrals where appropriate.

REFERENCES

Amato, J. A. II. (1982). *Guilt and gratitude*. Westport, CT: Greenwood Press.

Belgum, D. (1963). *Guilt: Where religion and psychology meet*. Englewood Cliffs, NJ: Prentice-Hall.

Bible, Holy (Revised Standard Version) (1953). New York: Thomas Nelson and Sons.

Bier, W. C. (Ed.). (1971). *Conscience: Its freedom and limitations*. New York: Fordham University Press.

Clark, C., & Finnelly, W. (1901). *The English reports* (House of Lords, Vol. 10, Session 1843–44). Edinburgh: William Green & Sons, p. 719.

Clyne, P. (1973). *Guilty but insane: Anglo-American attitudes to insanity and criminal guilt*. London: Thomas Nelson and Sons.

Drakeford, J. W. (1967). *Integrity therapy*. Nashville, TN: Broadman Press.

Eberhard, W. (1967). *Guilt and sin in traditional China*. Berkeley, CA: University of California Press.

Insanity (in criminal law). (1978). *The New Encyclopaedia Britannica* (Micropaedeia), (15th ed.), 5, pp. 367–368.

Freud, S. (1961). *Civilization and its discontents*. New York: W. W. Norton.

Gunn, H. E. (1978). *Manipulation by guilt: How to avoid it*. Waukegan, IL: Greatlakes Living Press, Ltd.

Knight, J. A. (1969). *Conscience and guilt*. New York: Appleton-Century-Crofts.

McKenzie, J. G. (1962). *Guilt: Its meaning and significance*. New York: Abingdon Press.

Mowrer, O. H. (1961). *The crisis in psychiatry and religion*. New York: Van Nostrand.

Ross, A. (1975). *On guilt, responsibility and punishment*. Berkeley, CA: University of California Press.

Wilhelm-Hooijbergh, A. E. (1954). *Peccatum: Sin and guilt in ancient Rome*. Groningen: J. B. Wolters.

Psychotherapy as a Process of Value Stabilization

JEFF SCHWEHN
CANDACE GARRETT SCHAU

VALUES ARE THE sinew of human society, and in the absence of a viable value system, culture collapses and simply ceases to exist (Kluckhohn & Strodtbeck, 1961). Values function as a system of enhancers and suppressors designed to affect behaviors a society deems supportive or menacing. Psychotherapy is a culturally endorsed medium that acts to define and transmit a societally designated value array designed to promote individuals' psychic well-being (Rieff, 1966). Psychotherapists serve as sanctioned purveyors of authorized values and assist clients' efforts to regain a meaningful sense of reality.

Until mid-century, psychotherapy endeavored to be identified as a scientific activity wherein a scientifically trained, objective expert provided empirically derived information to individuals in psychic need. Because science was viewed as neutral, value-free sets of proven constructs, the authoritative view of psychotherapy contended that psychotherapists observe client symptoms and dispense tested techniques to relieve client suffering (Andrews, 1987).

Against the dominant opinion, a persistent minority challenged the assumption of "value-free" psychotherapy by emphasizing the subtle but crucial role of values in the psychotherapeutic process (Glad, 1959). Starting in the mid-1950s, experimental investigation of the role of values in psychotherapy began to confirm that a significant value interchange occurred between therapist and client (Parloff, Iflund, & Goldstein, 1960; Petrony, 1966; Rosenthal, 1955). Early reviews of research into the effects of values in psychotherapy (Kessel & McBrearty, 1967; Kornreich & Meltzoff, 1970) concluded that therapists communicate their value preferences to clients; clients respond differentially to these value declarations; during the course of psychotherapy, clients shift their value configurations to more closely resemble those of their therapists; and client value convergence is positively related to beneficial treatment outcome.

Investigations of the conditions under which client-to-therapist value shifting occurred revealed a curvilinear relationship between initial client-therapist value similarity and beneficial outcome; too little or too much initial similarity was not associated with client change, whereas a modest amount of initial value congruence seemed to yield the greatest client value shift

(Cook, 1966; Parloff, Waskow, & Wolfe, 1978). Subsequent research has not successfully isolated the amount or specificity of initial value similarity sufficient and necessary for client change (Arizmendi, Beutler, Shanfield, Crago, & Hagaman, 1985; Beutler, 1981).

It may be more heuristic to assume with Frank (1973) that therapists and clients adhere to the same worldview or value system and that this common value ground serves as the relatively permanent structure of psychotherapy. In fact, Beutler's (1979) review of experiments on therapist and client value exchange during psychotherapy ascertained that, in large measure, therapists and clients agree on fundamental values. The critical, change-inducing variable between therapists and clients may be the greater relative stability of therapists' values in comparison with those of their clients (Katz & Beech, 1980). This relative therapist value stability creates the authority toward which value-unstable clients move for reassurance (Frank, 1973; Strong & Claiborne, 1982). In this model, psychotherapeutic change becomes, then, a process of client value stabilization in the presence of a value-stable expert within the framework of a shared value system.

There has been no research to substantiate therapists' relative value stability over the course of psychotherapy and little research on experienced therapists' or their clients' value changes in field settings (Beutler, 1983). This study investigates the value stability of practicing psychotherapists with more than 5 years postgraduate degree experience and their clients across the period of psychotherapy. We expect that therapists will be more value stable during psychotherapy than their clients will be. Additionally, we anticipate that, over the course of therapy, clients will realign their value systems to more closely resemble those of their therapists.

METHODOLOGY

Sample

Participants in the study were 13 employed, practicing psychotherapists from Colorado and New Mexico and 62 of their clients. Experienced therapists were recruited from a variety of helping professions including clinical psychology, counseling psychology, psychiatry, psychiatric nursing, pastoral counseling, and social work to provide a range of educational backgrounds and current therapy settings. The therapists (seven women, six men) were White with a mean age of 45.5 years (range: 39 to 64 years). All clients (39 women, 23 men) were involved in therapy with one of the therapists. Forty-two were White; 14 were Hispanic; 3 were Black; and 3 were American Indian. The mean age of the clients was 30.7 years (range: 19 to 61 years).

Instruments

Two instruments were used to tap the values construct. The Rokeach Value Survey (RVS), a self-administered instrument developed from fields surveys, literature, and personal interviews, asks each respondent to rank in order of importance to him or her two distinct lists of values. One is a compilation of 18 instrumental, or means to end-states of existence, values (e.g., Honest, Loyal, and Courageous), and the other is a group of 18 terminal, or end-states of existence, values (e.g., A Comfortable Life, A World at Peace, and Mature Love). These two ordinally ranked sets of values constitute the measure of therapist and client value systems (Rokeach, 1973). The RVS was chosen because of its relative ease and quickness of administration, its nonintrusiveness in the therapy process,and its widespread use in studying value change during psychotherapy (Rokeach & Regan, 1980).

The confidence rating scale (CRS) was developed to measure the confidence level of therapists and clients in their value rankings on the RVS. Immediately on completion of the RVS, therapists and clients were asked the following single item: "Right now, how confident are you that your rankings really reflect your values?" They responded on a 6-point scale ranging from *extremely confident* (1) to *extremely unconfident* (6); thus, lower scores indicate greater confidence.

Procedures

At the beginning of the study, all participating therapists completed and returned anonymous, initial versions of the RVS and CRS. After returning their measures, therapists invited each new client thereafter to join the study until between four and six clients per therapist were recruited. Before beginning treatment, each client completed and returned an anonymous, initial RVS and CRS. At treatment termination or at the end of a designated 6-month period, whichever came first, each client completed and returned an anonymous, final RVS and CRS. At the conclusion of the 6 months, all therapists completed and returned anonymous, final versions of the RVS and CRS. The 6-month period was selected because 75% of therapeutic change is achieved by this juncture (Howard, Kopta, Krause, & Orlinsky, 1986).

In this fashion, 13 completed sets of the RVS and CRS from therapists and 62 sets from clients were collected. All participants had read and signed an informed consent form prior to beginning the study.

Analyses

To examine value stability, prevalue (initial version) and postvalue (final version) ranking scores for therapists and for each therapist's set of clients were required. Each therapist's terminal and instrumental value rankings were obtained directly from their completed versions of the RVS.

An "average client" ranking score for each terminal and instrumental pre- and postvalue on the RVS was needed for each therapist's set of clients. To obtain these two sets of pre- and postvalue rankings, each client's RVS-ranked value position was noted separately for the 18 terminal and 18 instrumental values, both pre- and posttreatment. These value positions then were summed for each therapist's set of clients. Each terminal and instrumental pre- and postvalue position sum was divided by the number of clients in that set to yield a client mean ranking score for each value. An average client terminal and instrumental pre- and postvalues rank order was derived by listing the values in the rank order of the mean scores and assigning that rank order to the corresponding value. In this manner, an average client ranking for each terminal and instrumental pre- and postvalue was determined for each therapist's set of clients.

The formula for the Spearman rank-order correlation coefficient, which is frequently used with RVS responses, is derived from that for the Pearson Product Moment (PPM) correlation coefficient. Following Harris (1985), we elected to use the PPM correlation coefficient to establish stability levels across therapy (before and after) and congruence levels between therapist and corresponding average client. Fisher's z transformation of r was used whenever differences in correlation coefficients were tested (Snedecor & Cochran, 1967).

Dependent t tests were used to examine mean changes in the confidence levels expressed by therapists and average clients in their RVS rankings before and after therapy. Alpha levels of .05 and .01 were used in all analyses.

RESULTS

As expected, therapists' value systems were very stable across therapy (for terminal values, mean $r=.91$, *variance shared*=.83, range from .74 to .97; for instrumental values, mean $r=.91$, *variance shared*=.83, range from .82 to .95). Average clients' value systems were less stable and much more variable (for terminal values, mean $r=.55$, *variance shared*=.30, range from −.24 to .91; for instrumental values, mean $r=.53$, *variance shared*=.28, range from 0.1 to .79). Less than 20% (2 of 13) of the average clients' pre- and postrelationships for terminal values were stronger than the least stable therapist's pre- and postterminal value relationship. All of the average clients' pre- and post-relationships for instrumental values were weaker than that of the least stable therapist pre- and postinstrumental value relationship.

As hypothesized, the stability of therapists' terminal pre- to postvalues (mean $r=.91$) was significantly stronger than that of the average client (mean $r=.55$, $z=6.25$, $p<.01$). Similarly, the stability of therapists' instrumental preto postvalue rankings (mean $r=.91$) was significantly stronger than that of the average client (mean $r=.53$, $z=6.40$, $p<.01$).

Furthermore, to examine the stability of therapists' and clients' value systems to those of "normal" people, the pre- to postcorrelations from this study were contrasted with the RVS test-retest reliability coefficients, .71 for terminal values and .68 for instrumental values (Rokeach, 1973). As anticipated, average clients were less stable than the Rokeach norms (terminal: $z=-3.77$, $p<.01$; instrumental: $z=-3.34$, $p<.01$). On the other hand, therapists were more stable than the Rokeach norms (terminal: $z=8.73$, $p<.01$; instrumental: $z=9.47$, $p<.01$).

Also as hypothesized, the congruence between therapist and average client on terminal values obtained after therapy ($r=.69$, *variance shared*$=.48$) was significantly stronger than that measured before therapy ($r.=36$, *variance shared*$=.13$, $z=3.31$, $p<.01$). Similarly, the congruence between therapist and average client on instrumental values obtained after therapy ($r=.81$, *variance shared*$=.66$) was significantly stronger than that measured before therapy ($r=.33$, *variance shared*$=.11$, $z=5.47$, $p<.01$).

The results from the CRS scale support these RVS findings. There was a significant, average-client mean value confidence rating increase from pretherapy ($M=3.83$, $sd.=57$) to posttherapy ($M=2.75$, $sd=0.43$), dependent $t(12)=8.52$, $p<.01$, *effect size*$=2.36$. Therapists' mean prevalue confidence rating ($M=2.08$, $sd=0.64$) was significantly greater than the average clients' mean prevalue confidence rating ($M=3.83$, $sd=0.57$), dependent $t(12)=7.26$, $p<.01$, *effect size*$=-2.01$. Finally, therapists' mean postvalue confidence rating ($M=1.92$, $sd=0.64$) was significantly greater than their average clients' mean postvalue confidence rating ($M=2.75$, $sd=0.43$), dependent $t(12)=-3.64$, $p<.01$, *effect size*$=-1.01$.

DISCUSSION

The results of this field study suggest that psychotherapy can be viewed as a process of value stabilization for clients. Therapists in this study were more value stable than their clients across therapy. Therapists' rankings for both types of values before and after therapy were very similar, whereas their clients' rankings varied widely. Few of the average clients exhibited greater stability in their value rankings across therapy than did the least stable therapist. Therapists' average confidence level in their pretherapy rankings was much higher than that of their clients. Although therapists' mean confidence level after therapy still was higher, the gap between therapist and client confidence level had narrowed.

During psychotherapy, clients' values converged with those of their therapists. Therapists' and clients' value systems shared some similarities after therapy; before therapy, their rankings were quite distinct. Furthermore, clients were more confident of their value systems after therapy than they had been of their original pretherapy value systems.

In addition, these results indicate that practicing, experienced therapists and their clients represent unusual groups in regard to value stability. Therapists were more value stable than the RVS norm group, whereas clients were less stable.

More research is needed to determine and specify practical applications of the value stabilization model in the practice of psychotherapy. Replication of this investigation with a randomly selected population of therapists in outpatient and inpatient settings is crucial to extending the validity of the stability paradigm.

Arguably, the most valuable clinical expansion of the stability model would be a measurement of clients' therapeutic progress or lack thereof in relationship to their therapists' measured value stability. During psychotherapy, clients shift their values toward those of their therapists, and client value shifting occurs more than therapist value shifting; this value movement has been significantly associated with positive therapy outcome for clients (Beutler, Pollack, & Jobe, 1978). A next logical step would be an investigation of the link between therapist value stability and beneficial treatment effects for clients. By having therapists and their clients complete outcome measures, as well as Rokeach Value Surveys, it would be possible to determine if and how clients' improvement or deterioration varied with their therapists' value stability levels. These investigations could be constructed to ascertain if there is an optimal level of therapist value stability above which clients only improve marginally and below which clients suffer deleterious effects.

The impact of length of treatment also should be examined in regard to therapist value stability. There could be considerable practical benefit from knowing the time frames for client outcome enhancement in the presence of specified levels of therapist value stability. Almost certainly, societal funding sources would be interested in obtaining even a rough estimate of how quickly and pervasively certain therapists with specific levels of value stability could promote equilibrium in their clients' lives.

If it were shown that clients' well-being was significantly associated with delineated levels of therapist value stability, it would be ethically incumbent on the profession of psychotherapy to define the feeling and behavioral parameters of value unstable therapists. If the manifestations and limits of therapist value instability were clearly established, ethical guidelines could direct psychotherapists toward the proper courses of action to take in the event of significant value instability in their own lives.

REFERENCES

Andrews, L. M. (1987). *To thine own self be true: The rebirth of values in the new ethical therapy.* Garden City, NY: Anchor Press/Doubleday.

Arizmendi, T. G., Beutler, L. E., Shanfield, S. B., Crago, M., & Hagaman, R. (1985). Client-therpist similarity and psychotherapy outcome: A microscopic analysis. *Psychotherapy: Theory, Research, Practice*, 22(1), 16–21.

Beutler, L. E. (1979). Values, beliefs, religion and the persuasive influence of psychotherapy. *Psychotherapy: Theory, Research, Practice*, 16, 432–440.

Beutler, L. E. (1981). Convergence in counseling and psychotherapy: A current look. *Clinical Psychology Review*, 1, 79–101.

Beutler, L. E. (1983). *Eclectic psychotherapy: A systematic approach*. Elmsford, NY: Pergamon.

Beutler, L. E., Pollack, S., & Jobe, A. M. (1978). Acceptance: Values and therapeutic change. *Journal of Consulting and Clinical Psychology*, 46, 198–199.

Cook, T. E. (1966). The influence of client-counselor value similarity on change in meaning during brief counseling. *Journal of Counseling Psychology*, 13, 77–81.

Frank, J. D. (1973). *Persuasion and healing: A comparative study of psychotherapy* (2nd ed.). Baltimore: The Johns Hopkins Press.

Glad, D. D. (1959). *Operational values in psychotherapy*. New York: Oxford University Press.

Harris, R. J. (1985). *A primer of multivariate statistics* (2nd ed.). Orlando: Academic Press.

Howard, K., Kopta, S., Krause, M., & Orlinsky, D. (1986). The dose-effect relationship in psychotherapy. *American Psychologist*, 41(2), 159–164.

Katz, B., & Beech, R. P. (1980). Values and counselors, 1968–1978: Stability or change? *The Personnel and Guidance Journal*, 58, 609–612.

Kessel, P., & McBrearty, J. F. (1967). Values and psychotherapy: A review of the literature. *Perceptual and Motor Skills*, 25, 669–690.

Kluckhohn, F. R., & Strodtbeck, F. L. (1961). *Variations in value orientations*. Evanston, IL: Row, Peterson & Company.

Kornreich, M., & Meltzoff, J. (1970). *Research in psychotherapy*. Chicago: Aldine-Atherton.

Parloff, M. B., Iflund, B., & Goldstein, N. (1960). Communications of "therapy values" between therapist and schizophrenic patient. *Journal of Nervous and Mental Disorders*, 130, 193–199.

Parloff, M. B., Waskow, I. E., & Wolfe, B. E. (1978). Research on therapist variables in relation to process and outcome. In S. L. Garfield & A. E. Bergin (Eds.), *Psychotherapy and behavioral change: An empirical analysis* (2nd ed.) (pp. 233–282). New York: Wiley.

Petrony, P. (1966). Value change in psychotherapy. *Human Relations*, 19, 39–45.

Rieff, P. (1966). *The triumph of the therapeutic*. New York: Harper & Row.

Rokeach, M. (1973). *The nature of human values*. New York: Free Press.

Rokeach, M., & Regan, J. (1980). The role of values in the counseling situation. *The Personnel and Guidance Journal*, 58, 576–581.

Rosenthal, D. (1955). Changes in some moral values following psychotherapy. *Journal of Consulting Psychology*, 19, 431–436.

Snedecor, G. W., & Cochran, W. G. (1967). *Statistical methods* (6th ed.). Ames, IA: Iowa State University Press.

Strong, S. R., & Claiborne, C. D. (1982). *Change through interaction*. New York: Wiley.

Values and Ethics in Family Therapy

WILLIAM J. DOHERTY

FAMILY THERAPY EMERGED during the 1950s as a stepchild of psychoanalysis, cybernetics, and anthropology. After more than a decade of slow development as an alternative to traditional individual psychotherapies, family therapy spread rapidly during the 1970s to a position of widespread professional and popular acceptance. Like an energetic child, the family therapy movement in its early years concentrated on creating its unique identity in mental health professions. Only as the 1980s approached did leaders in the field begin to look inward at their professional values and ethical concerns.

This new interest in values and ethics can be traced to several developments occurring in the 1970s. First, the women's movement made it impossible for those in the family therapy field to ignore the implications of therapy for sex roles and women's equality (Hare-Mustin, 1980; Hines & Hare-Mustin, 1978). Second, the development of family therapy as a profession led to the development of a professional code of ethics promulgated by the American Association for Marriage and Family Therapy. Third, changing state laws concerning marriage, divorce, and parent-child relations, coupled with growing state regulation of marriage and family therapy, stimulated a new professional literature on difficult legal issues such as the family therapist's role in divorce and child custody conflicts (Kaslow & Steinberg, 1982; Ruback, 1982; Sporakowski, 1982). Fourth the research on negative effects of individual psychotherapy led to a similar concern in family therapy (Gurman & Kniskern, 1978).

These developments, in addition to the internal maturation of the family therapy field during its third decade, have produced a growing literature on values and ethics. In addition to works cited above, important contributions have been made by (a) Margolin (1982) in an overview article discussing thorny issues such as confidentiality, children's rights to consent to treatment, and therapist responsibility to different family members when their interests clash; (b) L'Abate (1982) in an edited volume covering a wide range of ethical and legal issues in family therapy; and (c) Jacobson (1983) in a critique of the implicit political values of behavioral marital therapy.

This *Counseling and Values* special issue attempts to move the professional dialogue on values and ethics a step further by "turning loose" a group of experienced and sophisticated family therapists on topics that they have thought about for many years. The goal of the issue is in-depth discussion of topics of special interest in the mid-1980s rather than comprehensive coverage of all the major values and ethical issues in the field.

THE CORE VALUES OF FAMILY THERAPY MODELS

The field of family therapy, like that of individual psychotherapy, has evolved into a variety of prominent models of therapy. Extending Schutz's fundamental interpersonal orientations (FIRO) theory of group development, Doherty and Colangelo (1984) proposed that family therapy models tend to differentially emphasize the dimensions of inclusion, control, and intimacy. Doherty and Colangelo defined *inclusion* as family interactions pertaining to membership, boundaries, individuality, belonging, and commitment; *control* as family interactions pertaining to power, influence, and decision making; and *intimacy* as family interactions pertaining to open self-disclosure, in-depth sharing, and close personal friendship.

After presenting this initial conception of the family FIRO model, Doherty, Colangelo, Green, and Hoffmann (1985) systematically analyzed chapters in Gurman and Kniskern's (1981) *Handbook of Family Therapy* to determine which FIRO dimensions are emphasized by the major family therapy models discussed. The best current source of comparative information on these models, Gurman and Kniskern's handbook presents 13 models of family therapy as described by developers of each model. A FIRO emphasis for each model was determined by a content analysis that rated the presence of the issue in the chapter (e.g., was intimacy discussed?) and the priority given to the issue in relation to other FIRO dimensions (e.g., if intimacy was discussed, was it given higher, lower, or the same priority as inclusion and control?). After performing this conceptual analysis of the chapters, the investigators sent their findings to the chapter authors for their feedback. The final ratings characterized the family therapy models according to their primary, secondary, and tertiary emphases.

The relevance of this material to values is as follows: I propose that the dominant assessment and treatment issue in a family therapy model reflects the dominant value underlying the model. In addition, I propose that the relative ranking of the FIRO dimensions represents the relative importance to the model of the corresponding values involved in the dimensions. What therapists pay attention to in therapy is more than a scientific or practical matter; they attend to what they believe is most important about human life and family relationships. If these assumptions are true, the rankings in Table 1 (derived from Doherty et al., 1985) reveal wide diversity among family therapy models in core values.

The major models listed in Table 1 divide fairly evenly in their primary emphases on the values of inclusion, control, and intimacy. For example, models such as Minuchin's structural family therapy give highest value to issues of belonging, membership, and subsystem clarity (inclusion); models such as strategic family therapy, behavioral marital therapy, and the Palo Alto interactional model singularly embrace the importance of control and influence in family relationships; and models such as Whitaker's symbolic experiential approach and Framo's psychoanalytically oriented family of origin approach place prime importance on the value of deep interpersonal exchanges (intimacy) in families.

A core value behind this family FIRO analysis is that of pluralism: Let a thousand flowers bloom and let us learn from our differences. Thus, my colleague Colangelo and I do not criticize any model of family therapy for emphasizing the "wrong" dimension of family life, because we believe that inclusion, control, and intimacy are all worthy aspects of family life. Viewing the family therapy models in this way, however, can shed light on the controversies and conflicts occurring in the field: Model differences reflect not only tactical or scientific differences but also divergence on cherished personal values about human relationships.

An example of the utility of this model is its application to perhaps the thorniest and most emotional ethical debate in the family therapy field: the ethics of using paradoxical or strategic interventions in therapy. These techniques, used extensively by strategic family therapists of the Haley, Palo Alto, and Milan models, involve covert manipulation by the therapist. Interventions include reframing the presenting problem in such a way that the identified patient is encouraged to continue with the symptomatic behavior so that the family stability is not undermined, and sometimes using a therapeutic team whose members pretend to disagree with one another

TABLE 1
Value Emphases of Thirteen Models of Family Therapy

Family Therapy Models	Family FIRO Issues*		
	Inclusion	Control	Intimacy
1. Open Systems Group-Analytic (Skynner)	2	3	1
2. Couples Contracts (Sager)	3	2	1
3. Family of Origin (Framo)	2	3	1
4. Contextual (Boszormenyi-Nagy & Ulrich)	1	3	2
5. Symbolic-Experiential (Whitaker & Keith)	2	3	1
6. Bowen Theory (Kerr)	1	3	2
7. Interactional (Bodin)	2	1	3
8. Structural (Aponte & Van Deusen)	1	2	3
9. Strategic (Stanton)	2	1	3
10. Functional (Barton & Alexander)	1	2	3
11. Problem-Centered (Epstein & Bishop)	2	1	3
12. Integrative (Duhl & Duhl)	2	3	1
13. Behavioral (Jacobson)	2	1	3

Note. Based on chapters in Gurman & Kniskern's (1981) *Handbook of Family Therapy.* *The *most important emphasis* (1); the *least important emphasis* (3).

and thereby force the family into a position of changing so that part of the therapy team can be proved wrong (Bodin, 1981; Stanton, 1981).

I believe that use of these strategic techniques as the core of a therapy model is consistent with a primary value emphasis on the control dimension of interpersonal relationships. Family relationships are based on control and influence; family members control one another through symptomatic behavior. This gridlock can be removed through ingenious counter-control techniques that render impotent the power of the symptom and thus allow the family to move more freely through its normal developmental course. Strategic therapists are ultimate pragmatists. They stress that their interventions work, and they answer charges that they are manipulators by freely acknowledging that all therapists manipulate their clients. Concealment of therapist intentions—the covert part of their manipulation—is not an ethical concern for these therapists, perhaps because disclosure of intentions reflects the value of intimacy, an issue that has low priority in strategic approaches to family therapy.

Family therapists who emphasize the intimacy aspects of family relationships, thereby embracing the value of subjectivity and open, honest self-disclosure, tend to be horrified at strategic interventions. In Whan's (1983) words: "Techniques of deception require a persona whose aim is concealment of intention. These covert manipulations are in a way a parody of the self-same secretive and Machiavellian relationships found in the psychopathologies of family life" (p. 335). A similar critique was offered by anthropologist Maranhao (1984), who accused strategic therapists of "dumping ... the ethical foundation of values, in their adherence to sophistic techniques of discourse" (p. 278). Maranhao went on to link the radical pragmatism of some family therapists to "a newly brewing worldview displayed by families themselves, according to which what is said is of lesser importance than what is accomplished" (p. 278). Intimacy-oriented therapist tend to be at the opposite end of the pragmatism continuum from control-oriented therapists, preferring to eschew self-conscious techniques to influence families because these techniques are thought to interfere with deep interpersonal connections—intimacy—in the therapy relationship and ultimately in family relationships.

Family therapists from different persuasions, then, are singing different anthems about families and family therapist interactions. The debate about strategic techniques could be enlightened by more careful delineation of core values underlying the therapy models of both proponents and opponents. On the one hand, it is ethically specious, in my view, to accept strategic interventions or any other interventions because they are thought to "work." If the criticism of these techniques is based on disagreements about values and ethics, then the decision to use them should be partly based on a careful judgment about their validity from the standpoint of ethics and values. On the other hand, criticisms of strategic approaches from intimacy-oriented therapists should clearly articulate the non-objective nature of the critique, namely, that it is based on differences in values rather than on any self-evident truths about human relationships and that reasonable, ethically sensitive people can disagree about these issues.

CONCLUSION

The emergence of self-analysis and self-criticism in the family therapy field signals a new level of maturity for the profession. Building on pioneering work already published, this article and this issue are intended to move this dialogue about values and ethics along the path of maturity. This path has no final destination with definitive answers, because human values and ethical concerns are continually renegotiated by each new generation. Still, there is hope for enough progress in the field that some of the current, major issues will someday be historical footnotes rather than still-controversial and still-painful concerns. My chief nominations for footnote status in a *Counseling and Values* special issue in 2085 are (a) the myth of value-free assessment and therapy, (b) the problem of sex stereotypes limiting the progress of women and men in family therapy, and (c) the issue of whether and under what circumstances strategic techniques are accepted as ethical in family therapy. In the meantime, the current task is to carefully consider professional values and respectfully debate ethical differences for the enrichment of counseling and family therapy professions.

REFERENCES

Bodin, A. M. (1981). The interactional view: Family therapy approaches of the Mental Research Institute. In A. S. Gurman & D. P. Kniskern (Eds.), *Handbook of family therapy* (pp. 267–309). New York: Brunner/Mazel.

Doherty, W. J., & Colangelo, N. (1984). The family FIRO model: A modest proposal for organizing family treatment. *Journal of Marital and Family Therapy, 10*, 19–29.

Doherty, W. J., Colangelo, N., Green, A., & Hoffmann, G. S. (1985). Emphases of the major family therapy models: A family FIRO analysis. *Journal of Marital and Family Therapy, 11*, 299–303.

Gurman, A. S., & Kniskern, D. P. (1978). Deterioration in marital and family therapy: Empirical, clinical and conceptual issues. *Family Process, 17*, 3–20.

Gurman, A. S., & Kniskern, D. P. (1981). *Handbook of family therapy*. New York: Brunner/Mazel.

Hare-Mustin, R. T. (1980). Family therapy may be dangerous to your health. *Professional Psychology, 11*, 935–938.

Hines, P. M., & Hare-Mustin, R. T. (1978). Ethical concerns in family therapy. *Professional Psychology, 9*, 165–170.

Jacobson, N. (1983). Beyond empiricism: The politics of marital therapy. *American Journal of Family Therapy, 11*, 11–24.

Kaslow, F. W., & Steinberg, J. L. (1982). Ethical divorce therapy and divorce proceedings: A psychological perspective. In L. L'Abate (Ed.), *Ethics, legalities, and the family therapist* (pp. 61–74). Rockville, MD: Aspen Systems.

L'Abate L. (Ed.). (1982). *Ethics, legalities, and the family therapist*. Rockville, MD: Aspen Systems.

Maranhao, T. (1984). Family therapy and anthropology. *Culture, Medicine, and Psychiatry, 8*, 255–279.

Margolin, G. (1982). Ethical and legal considerations in marital and family therapy. *American Psychologist, 37*, 788–801.

Ruback, R. B. (1982). Issues in family law: Implications for therapists. In L. L'Abate (Ed.), *Ethics, legalities, and the family therapist* (pp. 103–124). Rockville, MD: Aspen Systems.

Sporakowski, M. (1982). The regulation of marital and family therapy. In L. L'Abate (Ed.), *Ethics, legalities, and the family therapist* (pp. 125–134). Rockville, MD: Aspen Systems.

Stanton, D. (1981). Strategic approaches to family therapy. In A. S. Gurman & D. P. Kniskern (Eds.), *Handbook of family therapy* (pp. 361–402). New York: Brunner/Mazel.

Whan, M. (1983). Tricks of the trade: Questionable theory and practice in family therapy. *British Journal of Social Work, 13*, 321–337.

Therapist and Family Values in a Cultural Context

HOWARD F. STEIN

VALUES CONSTITUTE THE realm of standards in human conduct. Such standards are often deeply held and widely shared. They can find expression as fervent convictions, as situational appeals, as negative norms (in which violation is compliance), as deceptive veneer, as official pieties, and as clichés. One constantly make choices and judgments about the relative merit of alternatives without conscious awareness of the process (see Kluckhohn & Strodtbeck, 1961; Spiegel, 1971). As individuals, members of families, workers, and professionals, people live in accordance with shared meanings. It behooves social science professionals and clinicians always to assess the "mental status," "family function," and cultural significance of those proclaimed meanings (see Stein, 1985).

Values often feel like things that exist inside or outside oneselves, entities that people variously love, cherish, are committed to, feel driven by, and even feel appalled by ("I said *that*?"; "*That's* not me!"). Scheibe (1970) defined values as "what is wanted, what is best, what is preferable [and] what ought to be done" (p. 41). Values are not always consistently lived out, nor are they easily or often fully articulated. It is not enough to inquire into what a person, family, or group's (including professional group) values are (e.g., self-report), because one will invariably come up with an incomplete "shopping list" or series of "recipes" that hardly corresponds to how a person, family, or group actually lives. One must further inquire into the meanings or purposes those values serve (i.e., determine what these values are for in the system under consideration) (Kluckhohn & Strodtbeck, 1961; Spiegel, 1971).

Values constitute one aspect of that inner-representational world that shapes experience in terms of meaning, that conforms an outer "is" to an inner "ought to be." Values give coherence to inner- and outer-world alike—and to the movement between those realms. They also simultaneously separate that which is included in oneself from that which is excluded from oneself. Thus, they have a boundary-defining and boundary-maintaining function. Values affiliate "me" with "us" and disaffiliate "us" from "not-me" or "them." People not only use values to help them and to decide among choices but to help them constantly define who they are, whom they belong to, and who and what are to be regarded as outside.

An inquiry into the place of values in therapy is a tool that can enable therapists to understand the context in which one seeks to intervene, the standards one brings to that context, and how the interaction between the therapist and the family create yet a new context. By keeping the issue of values in mind as a diagnostic and strategic instrument, one may better be able to identify value differences (and their underlying meanings and consequences) between patient, family, and therapist(s) as a possible explanation for the failure of treatment to proceed at the rate or in the direction expected by its participant.

The clinical issue is not whether values affect the entire treatment process, but whether the clinician has access to how they do so, and in turn how the clinician can put into use knowledge of that process. Nothing so easily as counselors' and clinicians' unwitting commitments can seduce them into identifying and solving the wrong problem. The values of family, therapist, and of family therapy itself play a vital role in that clinical assessment that takes place reciprocally between clinician and family.

Let me identify at the outset my own theoretical proclivities. As a medical and psychoanalytic anthropologist and psychohistorian, I have found a psychoanalytic framework indispensable for understanding human behavior in families and in society. If, in this article, I seem to be a psychological and family determinist (which are, in my opinion, identical given the universal human biology of the sexed human body and of the family (see LaBarre, 1954/1968, 1972; Spiro, 1979, 1982) rather than a cultural determinist or cultural materialist, it is because external conditions (when one peers beneath the surface of consensus and myth) are more often pretexts and repositories for the emotional residue of childhood than they are causes for human behavior. Furthermore, to assert that culture is the source of values, families, and personalities is tautologous and thus fails to account for culture in the first place. For any therapy to be effective it must be meta-cultural (i.e., it must transcend collectively agreed-on ideological camouflages).

In culture, I argue, people get together to remember, repeat, and (optimally) work through their family experiences. Culture builds on and extrapolates from the unfinished business of family. When I speak of culture, I am using a shorthand to denote shared psychic and family organization. Certainly, although contrary to my own training and inclination, I can no longer accept a one-way cultural (or economic) determinisms: Culture is more heir than progenitor. In culture—and in cultural change over time which is history—individuals in groups constantly stage and replay what they have not resolved about their bodies and their families of origin (Binion 1981; deMause 1974; Stierlin, 1976; Volkan & Itzkowitz 1984). Values that groups share are living footprints of the members' formative family experiences. What psychoanalytic anthropologists and psychohistorians are discovering is how profoundly culture is heir to the family environment of infancy. Indeed, people adopt and shape that outer world of circumstance and history to conform with and conform the inner-representational world. The reader interested in further exploring this intellectual and clinical perspective is referred to such quarterlies as the *Journal of Psychohistory*, the *Journal of*

Psychoanalytic Anthropology, the *Psychoanalytic Review*, *American Imago*, and the annual *Psychoanalytic Study of Society*.

FAMILY LANGUAGE AND VALUES

Attention to a family's language often discloses those values it lives by, values that in turn shed light on how family members view one another and the family "itself." Many families depict themselves in terms of an economic metaphor. Parents may speak in terms of their emotional "investments" in their children, and the implicit outcome that they hope will follow, namely, the expectation of repayment with "interest," that is, a "return" on their investment. Children thus implicitly become something of "savings accounts" or "safety deposits boxes," so to speak, in which parts of the family's selfhood and future are put for safekeeping. As a result, the child becomes a container for parental wishes, ideals, and ambitions (e.g., achievement). Doctors and other therapists, too, often unwittingly feel the same about their patients, who become repositories of the therapist's own investments rather than distinct persons. When a child, patient, or family becomes "like money in the bank," child-rearing and therapy, respectively, may have the latent value of a counterphobic defense against separation anxiety.

To use a different example, Anglo-American familism permits wide geographic mobility within an accepted definition of *closeness*, whereas "Mexican-American extended familism . . . is anchored on geographic stability" (Keefe, 1984, p. 69). In identifying value orientations in any culture (e.g., associated with closeness), it is essential that observers and therapists alike elicit how they use their terms. Otherwise observers and therapists distort their informant's or client's reality by conforming it to their own unexamined values.

THE LOCATION OF VALUE JUDGMENT

The act of valuing something, consciously or unconsciously, always involves a value judgment (i.e., there is a heavy influence from the superego, either in its ego ideal aspect or its conscience aspect or a combination of both). One aspires to be or to do something; one is anxious in case he or she does or fails to do something. One may or may not, however, experience oneself to be the source of the value judgment. In clinical work, as in research, it is as crucial to observe and inquire where the particular experienced value is located (source, object) as it is to determine what constitutes the content of the value.

The value judgment might not originate in one's own eyes, but from the eyes of the external observer. One does not feel guilt in the sense of having formally internalized values but feels seen and caught and thereby shamed by something external to the self. What is more, the judgment of others may matter only when it exposes oneself (see Sharabi & Ani, 1977). Consideration of the question "Where does a given person perceive the value judgment to occur?" could serve as a valuable clinical tool for assessing boundaries within families.

TIMING AS VALUE IN THERAPY

People bring their assumptions and expectations to therapy about how and when things are "supposed to" unfold. Edward Hall (1977) has coined the term *action chain* to denote different peoples' preferred sequence of events and has traced much misunderstanding, ill feelings, and tragedy in human affairs to the failure to take one's own and others' action chains into accounts. The following vignette does not describe an actual single case but has come to be a type of case-within-a-case that I have seen occur between a Black patient (or family) and a White therapist.

> A Black female and her family enter therapy with a White counselor. The family find the therapist (more often a man than a woman) to be congenial, warm, and eager to help. Long before they are ready to make disclosures about family troubles, however, he wants to get down to business, to make the most of the time available, and begin to initiate some changes in the family's interactions. The family still likes him, but begins to find him intrusive, manipulating, and authoritative.
>
> Although the therapist expects investment in therapy to be rapidly forthcoming, the family is are more tentative. They may contrive small crises or situations in which the therapist will first have to prove himself to them. The therapist feels overwhelmed by the family's frequent use of the word "love" to describe not only how they feel about one another but—increasingly—about him. He feels enveloped into a present-time (almost timeless) sense of "being," while he wants to get down to the business of "doing" (future oriented). The family feels overwhelmed by the therapist's apparent attempt to change them.
>
> It did not take long for the family to feel abandoned, rejected, misunderstood; some of their misgivings about Whites were confirmed. It also did not take long for the therapist to develop parallel feelings. Where the respective "action chains" were left unaddressed, therapy often went nowhere or was suddenly terminated by the family (leave before you are left?). Although the issue of family-resistance to therapy does not dissolve in the face of these differences between family therapist and family, it certainly does not account entirely for the failure of therapy. The therapist will often assuage his own conscience by rationalizing the failure entirely on the basis of the family's resistance to therapy even though the therapist's unwitting resistance to the family has contributed to that picture.

My intention in offering this cumulative case is not to argue fatuously that attention to action chains would have solved the entire problem. Rather, it is to acknowledge that counselors and therapists constrain as well as are constrained in therapy and that they are limited by what they do not know. One can often best lead in therapy by demonstrating a willingness to follow the family's lead (i.e., an interest in experiencing the family "from within" so that one can change it). In therapy, timing is a value-laden issue for patient, family, and therapist alike.

RELATIVISM

Although it is mandatory that counselors and therapists calibrate particular family and therapist values in the context of the culture in which they occur, the mere fact of culture does not fully account for the meaning, use, and vicissitudes of values. Culture does not explain man; man explains culture. Friedman (1980) argued that the family crucible is the decisive context in which values and anything else that is cultural are shaped and given this meaning. "Customs, ceremonies, and values which usually are focused upon as causes of ethnic commitment operate really only at the service of the family emotional system" (p. 18). "Cultural camouflage is a universal emotional phenomenon" (p. 18). Finally, "Rather than supplying the determinants of family dynamics, *culture and environment supply the medium through which family process works its art*" (p. 20). In both family and therapist explanation, culture is often the focus of explanation by displacement, one that is then attributed the cause of the behavior under discussion. This is but another way in the human repertoire of transferring responsibility from "self" to "non-self" or environment (see Bidney, 1947, for discussion of the relationship between human nature and culture; see also Devereux, 1980; La Barre, 1968, 1972; Spiro, 1982; Stein, 1983, 1985).

Many clinicians and anthropologists commit what might be termed a *fallacy of exoticism*, the logic of which argues that the more bizarre or exotic appearing a cultural item (value) is, the greater the absolute distance between that person (or that person's culture) and the observers or clinicians. Clinicians and researchers must avoid the dual temptations of rationalizing away the unfamiliar into a more comfortable scheme and distancing themselves from the uncanny by making it into something bizarre or exotic (see Devereux 1967). Stated differently, fascination with the patient's culture may serve as the counselor or therapist's resistance to understanding the significance for himself or herself of the patient's or family's problem. The patient or family in turn may willingly comply with the clinician's pseudoethnographic interest both for narcissistic reasons (exhibitionism) and for resistance to therapy that parallels the reasons of the therapist. Thus, culture becomes used as a detour from therapy.

For example, from his experience in India, psychoanalyst Sudhir Kakar (1982) wrote that although Indian culture defines a person in terms of his or her relationships and "the fear of separation and loss is considered the most legitimate of human anxieties" (p. 274), it is unwarranted to conclude that the only appropriate therapy is identification with a traditional guru and thereby society. This would be taking cultural values at their face value rather than assessing them in their dynamic context as well: one that includes their profound cost. The guru-disciple relationship achieves internationalization of the guru at the price of never working through the dread of loss, an Indian variation on a universal principle of healing by symbolization, instead of coming to terms with what is symbolized. Kakar wrote:

> From my own experience of Hindu patients (and others), I find that in spite of the Indian cultural highlighting of the individual and the relational, the patients are more individual in their unconscious than they realize and often seek out Western-style psychotherapy in order to be comfortable with their individual strivings and needs. Conversely, it is quite conceivable that in spite of the Western cultural emphasis on autonomous individuality, the Western patients are more relational in their unconscious than *they* realize. (p. 275)

The very society that warns "don't fence me in" was identified by de Tocqueville and generations of America-observers after him as being a nation of inveterate joiners (voluntary associations, voluntarism—although more for social service than emotional intimacy).

Just as researcher and therapist may unwittingly perceive the informant or patient (family) as similar to oneself ("They're just like me") to minimize real differences, the researcher and therapist may also inadvertently exaggerate visible or stated differences and thereby fail in empathy ("You are too different from me, so I cannot identify with you"). Both are properly identifiable as countertransference issues rather than strictly patient or family issues.

Values and therapies themselves might be regarded as evolving historically and culturally. Moreover, such evolution cannot be automatically ascribed to economic, historical, or other environmental conditions (Badcock, 1980; deMause, 1982, Hippler, 1977). Only as one develops the capacity to experience and to value people (infants, spouses, those of differing ethnicities) as separate from oneself with needs and anxieties of their own, does he or she begin to define as "problems" or "pathologies" behaviors previously taken for granted as expected if not also sanctioned (e.g., historical infanticide, abuse). Therapists, too, have at least an implicit value theory (call it developmental or family functional) that to some degree matches their psychohistorical maturity. Accordingly, the therapist hopes to foster a diminution of externalization-projection between members of a family, and thereby an internalization and resolution of conflict; hopes to foster greater personal integration and a diminution of primitive splitting (i.e., people who are perceived as all-good and others who are perceived as all-bad); aspires to transform a family's silent and deadly somaticization and acting out into verbalization and the experiencing and articulation of feeling; and hopes to enable family members to experience and value one another more as distinct persons and less as containers or repositories for their own bad parts and idealizations.

EXAMPLE OF MIDWESTERN AMERICAN VALUES

In this section, I consider the midwestern American values within the context I have worked for the past 8 years. They illustrate how any cultural-regional values serve as clinical constraints and levers, the subtlety one must employ in identifying values at various levels, and the patience one must have (especially with oneself as researcher and clinician both) to identify subtle, implicit values as well as those that are manifest and those that can be verbalized: a distinction not available through administration of a values questionnaire.

Among many midwestern farming families, one's respectability in the eyes of the community—one's standing in terms of how one is viewed by others—is of paramount concern. Such a value often militates against one seeking therapy in the sense of individual or family exposure of problems to another in the community. Many are afraid to be seen in the office or clinic or anyone associated with mental health. On the other hand, in addition to the fear of public disclosure and thereby shame, there is the fear of disrupting one's relationships at home. To resolve the problem may be to have lost the relationship, and despite the value placed on personal autonomy, to a great extent the family comes first not only as an economic enterprise (Bennett, 1982) but as a very interdependent emotional system.

In the Midwest, indirectness and understatement ensure that one will save face, that one will maintain a safe distance from another. One goes to considerable lengths to avoid making direct demands on another, of doing anything that would seem to create conflict or threaten the delicately choreographed harmony. For instance, at a friend's home some months ago, the wife had cooked an elaborate meal of egg casserole, bacon, sausage, biscuits, and gravy. The gravy was near the end of the table at which I was seated. I had just spooned some onto my biscuits. Her husband said with something of a sparkle, "The gravy sure goes good with the biscuits, don't it?" I replied a complementary "Yes" and started eating. He then said with a smile, but now with more animation in his voice, "You mind sharin' some and passin' it down this way?" I passed the gravy, only the realizing the implicit request in the earlier, seemingly rhetorical question. "Peace at any price" is a widely held midwestern value.

Among midwestern families, a "united front" is viewed as essential to preserve the family reputation, to keep discord or dirt from being available to sully the image of the family. Loyalty to family secrets is the greatest guarantor of this united front. Midwestern Americans who pride themselves on defiant independence of thought also have a tender spot for how others view them. The protect themselves in counseling or therapy by saying little that could put their family in a bad light or be construed by the therapist as criticism of one another. I have found that lurking behind the public mask of equanimity is a fear of one's own aggression (often taking the form of loss of control) and the associated fear of separation (of doing irreparable damage through one's unacceptable anger). I have learned (as many midwestern individual and family therapists with whom I have talked have also learned) to honor the family myth and it function in conferring on the family protective distance from humiliating exposure. They expect the therapist to mirror themselves at their worst, akin to their formative experiences or the most negative denunciations from their churches. They feel a need for protection from themselves. They only gradually allow their secret vulnerabilities to surface. In the idiom of the region, they feel most secure when given "a lot of rope."

Patients, clients, or families will often rank values differently from the way counselors or therapists do so. In the wheat belt of the American Midwest, families will almost invariably choose completion of the harvest over jeopardizing harvest by taking time off to seek medical care, even in life-endangering situations. In this respect at least, farming families tend to value the continuity and integrity of the family and farm over the survival or health of the individual family member (Stein, 1982; Stein & Pontious, 1985). Although the health practitioner may rank health in the highest position and family or occupation lower in priority, many wheat-farming families do precisely the reverse.

The personal and clinical consequences of such rankings are interesting. On the one hand, clinicians often become perplexed to find that they and their patients do not always think and act alike (the extension of the self-model to the world). On the other hand, the experience of value (and other) difference often feels like an affront to which the clinician often responds by "digging in" deeper into his or her own rationale and rejecting the patient or family.

The clinician, who must be a relativist to be able to stand in the patient's and family's shoes, must also be one who is capable of taking a stand by example in behalf of values that may diverge widely from those of client, family, or society. Sometimes it is only the clinician—certainly not the family or society—who can make a claim in behalf of reality, intimacy, and clear but good conscience. A point rarely made in the family therapy literature—with its emphasis on the therapeutic activism, on what the counselor may do—is the availability of the counselor or therapist as an object of new identification and thereby internal restructuring of psyche and family. Such a therapeutic function is much undervalued in both the family therapy movement and literature.

THERAPIST VALUES AND THE VALUE OF FAMILY THERAPY

Any discussion of the relationship between values and therapy must address the admittedly discomfiting question of "Whose values?" Therapists often speak loosely—and with resolve as well—about "the value of therapy (especially of family therapy)" and "the value of bringing the entire family together to meet." Very often I will say, "You need such and such," when what I really mean is: "I think you need, or I recommend, such and such." The transformation is revealing and disturbing, for it makes it seem as though I am not the source of the idea (i.e., the "need" that I locate in you) and, furthermore, as if my authority as clinician, teacher, or supervisor should make it self-evident to you what you need. The self-critical clinician will always be on the lookout for his or her own countertransference manipulations of patient or family, and will constantly be asking, "Am I making such and such an intervention for my own good or for the good or the patient (family)?"

Throughout 15 years of work with psychiatrist and family physician residents, I have heard the same painful, anxious, and angry outcry:

> Too much analysis is just paralysis. Don't just help me to understand the case. Tell me what to do, so that I can get in there, intervene, make things better quickly, and finish. All you leave me is impotence. Where does this leave me? This sort of analysis just makes things worse. I would rather *not* know so much. You end up not being able to do anything.

My response is to try to help them understand their compulsion to act (i.e., the inner and widely shared meaning of the value cluster of decisiveness, master, control, and winning) and thereby to help them to make a better-informed decision about what the problem(s) is and whose it is so that the clinician does not proceed to treat the patient or family for his or her own distress.

In recent years, technological, engineering, military, and sports metaphors have come to dominate clinical and managerial thinking alike. They convey not only an image of many but an ideal of what a good person, family, or group should be like: in short, a value. A veteran physician's associate colleague, fresh from triumphantly replumbing his entire house, lamented to me, "I wish I could fix people the way I fix pipes. Isolate the problem, take out what's defective, put in what works, and you're through." A value orientation, based exclusively on action, mastery, individualism, and the relentless pursuit of the future, commits those in the healing professions to frequently unrealistic reliance on one-way technique. Treatment becomes mere repair.

Patients, families, and therapists often collude in the illusion of control (i.e., whereby the more one does, plans, or acts, the more confident one feels, even though one confirms only the illusion of being in charge). Therapists need to act decisively. Their unwillingness to acknowledge that they are always working within the frameworks of others and the frequent feeling of defeat, if not personal inadequacy, when reality frustrates ambition are part of the cultural "baggage" of much of the family therapy movement over the past 2 decades. A moment's reflection will remind the therapist that much of what one had thought to be primarily a clinical value is in fact widely cultural; from that realization one has the option to implement cultural definitions or to approach them critically.

Such cultural values as self-reliance, autonomy, and individualism, which will enhance separateness, often serve as massive reaction formations and rationalizations against dependency wishes and fear of fusion. Similarly, generations of immigrants sought American freedom as a way of repudiating tenacious internal, family, and cultural ties in their homelands (and American regions) of origin. Steadfastly disengaged families have a curious habit of tracing back to steadfastly enmeshed ones. The temporal phasing can likewise go in reverse, as closeness is a way of making restitution for or undoing the real and fantasied hurts of independence, abandonment, and self-reliance. To be a penitential prodigal son or daughter, one must first have left with a flourish. Finally, having said all this, it is difficult for me to conclude that intimacy, the relationship grounded in a sense of a self that fosters the selfhood of another, is somehow located in the middle of a scale the very extremes of which are not only defenses against separation anxiety, but which are revealed to be far more complex than the popular enmeshment-disengagement model avows. Such a model may become a procrustean bed that conforms data to theory.

One might stop and inquire: "Why are we so interested in assessing and measuring families now?" A moment's reflection will remind us that since the turbulent late 1960s, the family has itself become the object of value. The family has even become the object of legislation in the effort to preserve it from dying or extinction. Value-laden ideological issues have profoundly influenced the family research and family therapy movements (see Saunder, 1979).

Culturally, the value of familism contrasts with the paired value of individualism: They have vied since the earliest refugees came from England to the Plymouth and Jamestown colonies. When Americans overly weighted the value of individualism, they "discovered" the family; now that the family has become the vogue ideologically, Americans find that they must "reinvent" the individual. If family therapy is to help guide American society through these culture-wide ideological spasms of anti-authority and authoritarianism, individualism and collectivism, rather than succumb to them, then it must first recognize them for what they are.

I have learned a great deal from patients and families about how to "do" therapy and how to teach it. I vividly remember working with an ambitious and successful businessman and his wife (later, with their two infants). For years, he strove to live up to his father's exacting and unfulfillable expectations, because his father, too, was a successfully, largely self-made businessman. During the course of therapy, he came to be able to acknowledge anger about his father, his intense disappointment with a father who could not provide love without a high-price ticket on it; he began to mourn rather than strive so uncompromisingly. Months into therapy, he said tearfully, "The bottom line is that there is no bottom line." With that insight he began to transcend the economic or business metaphor that had kept him in the captivity of his childhood.

He taught me much about the importance above all else of fostering in the meeting room a "holding environment" in which values might emerge. Therapy that is effective must be one in which the therapist allows his or her own world to become "topsy turvy" to hear the patient or family and thereby to respond to them. The result is as much a creation of the therapist as of the patient or family. And everyone is changed.

Und wir, die an steigendes Glück
denken, empfänden die Rührung,
die uns beinah bestürzt,
wenn ein Glückliches fällt. (p. 84)

And we, who have always thought
of happiness climbing, would feel
the emotion that almost startles
when happiness falls. (Rilke, 1939, p. 85)

REFERENCES

Badcock, C. R. (1980). *The psychoanalysis of culture*. Oxford, England: Basil Blackwell.

Bennett, J. W. (1982). *Of time and the enterprise: North American family farm management in a context of resource marginality*. Minneapolis: University of Minnesota Press.

Bidney, D. (1947). Human nature and the cultural process. *American Anthropologist, 49*, 375–399.

Binion, R. (1981). *Soundings: Psychoshistorical and psycholiterary*. New York: Psychohistory Press.

Cantril, H. (1960). *Soviet leaders and mastery over man*. New Brunswick, NJ: Rutgers University Press.

deMause, L. (Ed.). (1974). *The history of childhood*. New York: Psychohistory Press.

deMause, L. (1982). *Foundations of psychohistory*. New York: Creative Roots.

Devereux, G. (1967). *From anxiety to method in the behavioral sciences*. The Hauge, Netherlands: Mouton.

Devereux, G. (1980). *Basic problems of ethno-psychiatry*. Chicago: University of Chicago Press.

Erikson, E. H. (1968). *Identity, youth and crisis*. New York: Norton.

Ferreira, A. J. (1963). Family myth and homeostasis. *Archives of General Psychiatry, 9*, 457–463.

Friedman, E. H. (1980). The myth of the Shiksa. *The Family* (Center for Family Learning), *8*, 13–22.

Hall, E. (1977). *Beyond culture*. Garden City, NY: Doubleday/Anchor.

Hippler, A. E. (1977). Cultural evolution: Some hypotheses concerning the significance of cognitive and affective interpretation during latency. *Journal of Psychohistory, 4*, 419–438.

Kakar, S. (1982). *Shamans, mystics and doctors: A psychological inquiry into India and its healing traditions*. New York: Knopf.

Keefe, S. E. (1984). Real and ideal extended familism among Mexican-Americans and Anglo-Americans: On the meaning of "close" family ties. *Human Organization, 43*, 64–70.

Kluckholn, F., & Strodtbeck, F. (1961). *Variations in value orientations*. Evanston, IL: Row Peterson.

LaBarre, W. (1968). *The human animal*. Chicago: University of Chicago Press. (Original work published 1954).

LaBarre, W. (1972). *The ghost dance: The origins of religion*. New York: Dell.

Rilke, R. M. (1939). Tenth elegy. In J. B. Leishman & S. Spender (Trans.), *Duino elegies* (pp. 78–85). New York: Norton.

Sander, F. (1979). *Individual and family therapy*. New York: Aronson.

Scheibe, K. E. (1970). *Beliefs and values*. New York: Holt, Rinehart and Winston.

Sharabi, H., & Ani, M. (1977). Impact of class and culture on social behavior: The feudal-bourgeois family in Arab society. In L. C. Brown & N. Itzkowitz (Eds.), *Psychological dimensions of Near Eastern studies* (pp. 240–256). Princeton, NJ: Darwin Press.

Spiegel, J. (1971). *Transactions: The interplay between individual, family, and society.* New York: Science House.

Spiro, M. E. (1979). *Gender and culture: Kibbutz women revisited.* Durham, NC: Duke University Press.

Spiro, M. E. (1982). *Oedipus in the Trobriands.* Chicago: University of Chicago Press.

Stein, H. F. (1982). The annual cycle and the cultural nexus of health care behavior among Oklahoma wheat farming families. *Culture, Medicine and Psychiatry, 6,* 81–99.

Stein, H. F. (1983). An anthropological view of family therapy. In D. Bagarozzi, A. Jurich, & R. Jackson (Eds.), *New perspectives in marriage and family therapy: Issues in theory, research, and practice* (pp. 262–294). New York: Human Sciences Press.

Stein, H. F. (1985). Values and family therapy. In J. Schwartzman (Ed.), *Families and other systems* (pp. 201–243). New York: Guilford.

Stein, H. F., & Pontious, J. M. (1985). Family and beyond: The larger contact of non-compliance. *Family Systems Medicine, 3,* 179–189.

Stierlin, H. (1976). *Adolf Hitler: A family perspective.* New York: Psychohistory Press.

Volkan, V. D., & Itzkowitz, N. (1984). *The immortal Atatürk: A psychobiography.* Chicago: University of Chicago Press.

The Values of Counseling: Three Domains

EDWIN L. HERR
SPENCER NILES

THE COUNSELING PROFESSION has evolved from a stage in which some of its advocates professed to be value-free and scientifically detached from the values of clients (Walters, 1958) to a more realistic phase in which it is clear that any intervention in the life-space or lifestyle of people carries with it values implications or, indeed, promotes values (London, 1964). As Bergin (1985) suggested, "values are orienting beliefs about what is good for clients and how that good should be achieved" (p. 99). As such, values influence, and in fact permeate, counseling and psychotherapy, theories of personality and pathology, the design of change methods, the goals of treatment, and the assessment of outcomes. Other observers have indicated that client's values make up much of the "content" of counseling, while the values of the counselor enter into the "process" of counseling (Pietrofesa, Hoffman, Splete, & Pinto, 1978, p. 55).

Although, as the observations of Bergin (1985), London (1964), and Pietrofesa et al. (1978) attest, values applicable to counseling and psychotherapy in general have been discussed in the professional literature, it is less evident that values have been fully examined in relation to specific counseling emphases (e.g., the interactions between clients and counselors from differing ethnocultural backgrounds, career counseling, or with regard to national differences in counseling provisions). In each of these arenas, it can be assumed that the possible source of tensions between counselors and clients, counselors and institutions, or the providers of counseling services and the policy makers in certain nations, is a lack of explicitness in the values assumed by individual counselors, counseling approaches, or intervention theories.

The intent of this article is to briefly illustrate how values, as orienting beliefs about what is good for a client, groups of clients, or a nation, may affect the delivery of counseling.

THE ROLE OF VALUES IN COUNSELOR INTERACTIONS WITH CLIENTS

Numerous authors have noted that the counseling profession has historically been grounded in assumptions that are associated with a White Anglo-Saxon

Protestant world view (Sue, 1981; Warren, 1962). It has also been asserted that counselors functioning within this "world view" tend to prefer clients who are young, attractive, verbal, intelligent, and successful (YAVIS) (Schofield, 1964). Those clients not in possession of these attributes often receive inappropriate treatment and become disillusioned with the therapy process (Padilla, Ruiz, & Alverez, 1975). For the most part, this disillusionment is the result of unexamined values and preferences on the part of the counselor with regard to his or her own values and those of the client, especially as these values affect the treatment modality employed by the counselor.

Rather than considering the possibility that the counselor's values and the intervention strategy may run counter to the client's value system, therapists often label the client as "abnormal" or "unresponsive to treatment" (Buss, 1966). The bias of this mind-set can lead to destructive rather than constructive results for those clients who do not possess values that coincide with the therapist's values or with the values underlying a particular approach to therapy (Pine, 1972).

Within such a context, it is unfortunately often the case that the counselor does not understand the client's value system or its cultural antecedents. The absence of such understanding leads to a situation in which the counselor engages in the inappropriate labeling of client behavior rather than differential diagnosis. Based on such behavior, it is no wonder that a majority counselor-minority client match frequently leads to the premature termination of the counseling relationship by the minority client (Sue, 1977). A core condition of the therapeutic relationship, namely that of accurate empathy, has been grossly violated by the counselor (Rogers, 1951). Thus, it would seem that counselor insensitivity to client values and cultural mores often leads to inappropriate counseling interventions that, in turn, result in the exacerbation of the client's issues of concern rather than their alleviation.

Need for Counselor Awareness of Cultural Diversity

Sue (1983) urged the helping professions to acknowledge the shortcomings of attempting to resolve ethnic minority issues by using convergent reasoning in an attempt to arrive at "the solution." Sue argued for the incorporation of divergent reasoning in our attempts to gain cultural sensitivity. In other words, rather than forcing a dichotomy between *etic* (universal, all human beings are alike) and *emic* (cultural uniqueness and individual differences) perspectives, he advocated a synthesis of the two, emphasizing their complementarity in the attempt to understand human nature. This viewpoint is a departure from past tendencies to opt for singular definitions of culture and values with regard to the goals of counseling interventions. This approach may result in some discomfort because it requires the counselor to accept a certain degree of ambiguity by acknowledging the need for cultural pluralism rather than assuming the validity of generalizing a specific value system and world view to all clients.

Once this sensitivity is acquired, however, the counselor will be able to assist the client to more fully and openly pursue his or her own values and how they may relate to the issue of concern for the client. Both the counselor and the client will then be likely to proceed productively with the therapy process.

Within the broad parameters of cultural diversity, it is also necessary to acknowledge the potential tensions that arise from a socioeconomically middle-class counselor and a client of a different socioeconomic status. It can be argued that such conflict can occur when the counselor limits him or herself to viewing client behavior through a psychological lens that assumes individual action to be the prime determinant of success or happiness. In such a view, individual initiative, planfulness, deferred gratification, and achievement orientation may be values consciously or unconsciously imposed on the client by the counselor. In these situations, clients for whom such values are neither prized nor socially inculcated may be viewed as lazy, marginal, unmotivated, abnormal, or described using other such labels that are, in fact, value-laden rather than a result of valid, client-centered differential diagnosis.

In one sense, it can be argued that the counselor's view just described is a unidemensional psychological view. Counselors holding this view assume that unfettered individual action is available to all clients and that competition, achievement, and activity are goals and processes that signal maturity and positive mental health. But such a view does not reflect sociological perspectives. Sociological perspectives tend to argue less that persons can choose and behave unrestrained by environmental constraints and more that one's values are largely situationally determined (Roberts, 1981).

Sociological views also emphasize that the social structure represents the context in which each person negotiates his or her identity, belief systems, and life course. The social structure is the seed bed from which values emerge. Depending upon the social structure of which one is a part and the values to which one has been conditioned, client and counselor values may be quite similar or dramatically different. The point, of course, is not that value sets are in themselves normal or abnormal, they simply "are." As entities that shape and motivate individual behavior, value sets are a complex mix of individual psychology about the types of initiative and action that are appropriate, and sociological insights about the context that defines, permits, and reinforces or constrains such individual behavior. Unless such individual-environmental interaction is understood by a counselor, differential value sets and their relationships to cultural diversity are not likely to be fully appreciated as ways in which clients organize their personal reality.

THE ROLE OF VALUES IN COUNSELING STRATEGIES

Although the counseling process itself is affected by the interaction of client values and counselor values, intervention strategies and treatment modalities also carry value loadings that need to be reflected in counselor sensitivity. Two examples, psychometric approaches and career services, will serve to make the point.

Values in Assessment

As has been the focus of much controversy and debate in the past two decades, many assessment instruments are grounded in constructs and content that have an obvious culture-specific bias (Butcher & Pancheria, 1976). Cultural membership has much to do with how any individual interprets time and space and how he or she experiences reality. Cultural influences are, therefore, inevitably manifested in the individual's behavior. Because psychological assessments examine samples of this behavior, the cultural milieu of the individual will be reflected in his or her test performance. In this regard, Anastasi (1982) noted the following:

> Each culture fosters and encourages the development of behavior that is adapted to its values and demands. When an individual must adjust to and compete within a culture or subculture other than that in which he or she was reared, then cultural difference is likely to become cultural disadvantage. (p.286)

Therefore, what is considered to be an objective assessment instrument with some majority cultures many not be so with a minority group or persons from a cultural orientation different from that on which the instrument was standardized.

One reaction to the cultural bias in testing has been the attempt to develop "culture free" assessment methods. It is now acknowledged that the development of a "culture free" assessment instrument is an unachievable ideal. Each test that is developed will have the tendency to favor those individuals who are from the culture in which the assessment instrument was constructed. A more realistic goal is the attempt to create assessments that reflect constructs and content that are common across cultures, that is, an *etic* perspective as previously described. These types of assessments have been labeled as "culture-common," "cross-cultural," or "culture-fair" tests. By focusing on the commonalities within such variables as language, styles of expression, and content, the "culture clash" between examinee and exam can be minimized. For instance, an assessment that consistently uses a pictorial representation of a single racial type or a value system that reflects a particular socioeconomic class may serve to alienate an examinee who does not share the same racial or class background. Although "cross-cultural" assessment instruments will not completely eliminate cultural bias in measurement, they will serve to reduce this bias.

Although there are other issues that should be considered in exploring the role of values in psychometric approaches (e.g., examiner bias, normative bias), the overarching point of this discussion is that values assumptions are unavoidable components of every assessment instrument. As constructs and content are defined and selected during the process of assessment construction, certain values are deemed as prized while others are discarded as being not relevant. In this regard, no single assessment is equally applicable to all cultures. Thus, test users must be sensitive to the ways in which the values of the client may negatively interact with values underlying respective assessment instruments to avoid bias in testing as well as the inappropriate use of assessment results.

Values in Career Services

A need to acquire a sense of the values inherent in an intervention strategy is, perhaps, in no case more important than in that of career services. There are two major values issues involved here. One has to do with the nature of the values inherent in career services themselves, whether career guidance, career education, or career counseling, and in their instrumental character as a purveyor or confronter of value sets. The other issue has to do with the cultural and socioeconomic value sets that may attend the provision of career services.

In a major sense, the propositions that define the various career services are activist, not passive, strategies. The underlying value sets reflect such activism. Career interventions expect persons to value work, to plan, to be purposeful, to be productive, to be serious about life's meaning, to be useful, and to be committed to growth and learning rather than to passively accept being unemployed or on welfare. More specifically, perhaps, career services implicitly or explicitly require that schools and agencies, counselors and clients, accept or reject the values inherent in what career services represent.

In speaking about career education, Swanson (1972) suggested the presence of several values issues in such a treatment modality. Among them are the distribution of society's tasks and roles, the work ethic, and the equality of opportunity.

Phenix (1973), too, pointed out the major significance and complexity of eight basic value issues associated with career education. Three of these deal with meaning, one with the human condition, one with time, and three with society. Phenix arrays these value issues using contrasting extremes such as work and play, change and permanence, equality and difference, unity and plurality, generalist and specialist, hierarchy and leveling, and the person and the collective.

Although career education is essentially a career service that is school based, the values issues described by Swanson and Phenix are not confined to the relationship between education and work. Rather, they extend value issues related to the provision of career services to fundamental matters both of social meaning related to work and to the purposes for which mechanisms to distribute workers across roles and tasks are to serve: individual fulfillment, human capital, or some combination of these. This matter will be discussed more fully in the final section of this article as national comparisons are made.

Cultural and Socioeconomic
Value Sets in Career Services

In addition to the broader social values that are inherent in how career services are defined and implemented, there are also the cultural and socioeconomic value issues that affect individuals. However these career services (e.g., counseling, guidance, education) are described, they require clients to confront their values, to make deliberate choices based on these values, and then to implement these values in a plan of action that will alter the conditions that occurred when they came to counseling.

At the individual level, as was suggested previously, it is crucial that counselors understand the potential impact of the environment on the career development of the client. The cultural milieu of the client serves to determine the points at which educational or occupational choices are made, the educational and occupational alternatives that will be considered or known to an individual, as well as the motive factors that the individual plays out in choices made. In large measure, the career choices made by individual clients are culture-specific and they are inextricably related to individual values.

The need to examine value issues in career services becomes increasingly evident as one realizes that every choice is ultimately a choice of value to be realized or served. As such, it is imperative that counselors recognize not only the values and assumptions that they themselves hold, but also that they realize that no counseling intervention is value free.

THE ROLE OF VALUES ACROSS NATIONAL COUNSELING MODELS

As the previous sections have suggested, values of counselors and clients interact in the individual counseling encounter, and different value sets characterize specific counseling emphases or techniques (e.g., career counseling). There is a third dimension of value effects that also needs to be considered. Various value sets are also related to the provision of counseling services within and across nations. In microcosm, research in cross-cultural counseling attests to the importance of value differences between culturally distinct persons and the effects these have for the counseling process (Marsella & Pedersen, 1981; Sue, 1983). The values issues implicit in cross-cultural counseling among dyads can, however, also be examined in macro-terms, at the level of nations.

The Values of Counseling: Three Domains

For the purposes of this article, we will consider only three possible issues that relate to differences in counseling in national terms, to the transportability of counseling theory and practices across national boundaries, and to the derivation of values within cultural groups. These issues will be discussed in reverse order.

The Derivation of Values within Cultural Groups

In the popular press and government statements, nations of the world are referred to as belonging to such categories as East and West, North and South, underdeveloped, developing, developed, Third World postindustrial, or by other such euphemisms. These terms are not simply geographic referents. Rather, they reflect the integration of political, economic, and psychological characteristics that, however imperfectly, distinguish nations in one category from another. What is less evident but equally true is that the types of national characteristics described in other terms reflected above are also manifested in values differences. The latter make up the social metaphors that individual nations play out, and are reflected in the idealized personality types that nations advocate and reinforce. Such preferred personality types are manifested in belief systems, art, philosophy, history, schooling, and other instrumentalities.

Kluckhohn (1951, 1956) and Kluckhohn and Stodtbeck (1961) were early researchers in examining value differences across cultures. Using specific categories of value sets (e.g., people-nature orientation, time orientation, activity orientation, relational orientation, and definitions of human nature as good, bad, or immutable), they found "within culture" similarities and "between culture" differences. More recently, Hofstede (1984) reported research findings showing value differences on four culture dimensions: power distance, uncertainty avoidance, masculinity versus femininity, and individualism versus collectivism. Each culture then uses its own instrumentalities of education and socialization to form social personalities that will fit into the set of values predispositions that dominate that society at a particular point in time. Individualism, community, freedom, achievement, compliance, loyalty to the group, patriotism, sacrifice, flexibility, tradition-directed, inner-directed, and other-directed are terms that combine differently in different nations to give substance to the "social metaphors" that make up the social and cultural identity to which citizens are expected to aspire (Vaisey & Clark, 1976). Placed in personal terms, "each individual is surrounded by a continually changing set of environmental conditions that influence him or her and force particular patterns of thinking and behaving" (Peterson, 1985, p. 124). It is this individual-environment transaction that is the seed bed for values formation and change. It is also the substance of the sets of environmental conditions that differentiate national thought and value sets.

Such differences are manifested not only in individual values, but also in attitudes toward counseling and mental health services.

National Perspectives on Counseling

Because counseling and mental health services are promoters of values (London, 1964), national government vary in their support for and expectations of such services. At issue here are the ways in which value assumptions within counseling tend to be swayed by the economic and political security of respective countries at particular moments in their history. Super (1983) noted that those countries that are relatively prosperous and free from outside intervention have the tendency to view counseling and other forms of guidance as a vehicle for furthering the enhancement of the individual's abilities, interests, and personal values. Conversely, it is the case that nations experiencing economic hardships or the possible threat of outside intervention tend to view counseling or guidance as a vehicle for directing youth into occupational endeavors that are deemed as being crucial for national survival. In discussing these tendencies, Super suggested the following:

> The goals of guidance and counseling will be determined by national policies, and those of us who value individual development must foster it with the means that are at our disposal despite the political climate. We must work on policy for its improvement and within policy for the preservation of humanistic values (p. 512).

Although Super (1983) offered this suggestion as a means by which the counselor can bridge the gap between individual freedom and national control with regard to values assumptions within counseling, the more basic point here is that one must first gain an awareness as to where respective counseling interventions fall on the individual-national value continuum.

As a result of studying national approaches to career guidance, Watts and Herr (1976) suggested that two dimensions could be identified that distinguish international approaches to helping youth and adults with their career development. The two dimensions can be differentiated in terms of (a) whether the primary focus of the national approach is on the needs of the individual or the needs of society, and (b) whether the approach basically accepts the status quo or is concerned with changing it in prescribed directions. Table 1 is a graphic illustration of these two dimensions.

One can conceive each of the cells in Table 1 as a value set that shapes a particular nation's provision of career guidance services through legislation, definitions of groups to be served, and expectations of appropriate questions, techniques, and outcomes. These value sets acknowledge that in every nation, counseling, career guidance, psychotherapy, and other mental health services are more or less sociopolitical processes that inadvertently or consciously reflect the values which that nation attributes to helping its citizens with various types of personal, career, or psychological problems. Thus, models of counseling services are significantly affected by the characteristics

TABLE 1
International Approaches to Helping Youth and Adults with Career Development

	Needs of Society	Needs of the Individual
Change	Social Change Approach (1a)	Individual Change Approach (1b)
Status Quo	Social Control Approach (2a)	Non-Directives Approach (2b)

of the society in which they are found because every counseling approach is in essence a form of environmental modification that in turn carries political overtones through the assumptions and value sets inherent in each approach.

Beyond the level of influence that values have on the availability and the shape of counseling provision in each nation, it is also obvious that the content of the counseling interaction depends on the individual client's perception of, conflict with, or unclarity about (a) values held by others, (b) values expected of the individual by various institutions or choice options, or (c) values that the person feels necessary to guide his or her present or future action. Under any model of counseling or career guidance, it is possible to argue that the types of questions that youths and adults bring to counselors are a function of how they view current societal belief systems about such matters as personal choice, achievement, role differentiation, social obligation, and many other aspects of life. The resulting anxieties, deficits, or indecisiveness that these people experience as they compare themselves with what society's agents (e.g., parents, teachers, employers, spouses, mass media) say they should believe or do represents a large part of the content with which counselors deal (Herr, 1982). These are basically values questions.

To return to Table 1 briefly, the point is that each of the cells in the model reflect a national value set that might be attributed to counseling services. For example, cell 1a could reflect a value that argues that counseling services should be devoted to creating human capital, a literate work force that needs to be channeled into those areas of occupational need experienced by a nation in its current form of economic development. Cell 1b could represent a value set that epitomizes counseling services devoted to facilitating individual free choice and purposeful action, promoting decision making, and self-actualization. In some contrast, cell 2b may also value needs of the individual, but take a much more benign approach to what occurs in career guidance, permitting such services to respond to whatever individual needs tend to arise. Cell 2a may be less concerned with creating human capital for emerging development, and more concerned with national needs to preserve a class structure that defines the opportunity limits within which individuals will be informed and encouraged. Thus, each cell reflects both a national social metaphor and a national model of the appropriate "social personality" that counseling services are to encourage. Each cell also suggests a valued counselor type: 1a, identifier and channeler of talent; 2a, gatekeeper; 1b, maximizer; and 2b, problem solver. The notion of Table 1 as a structure composed of national value sets could be extended to other organizations of mental health services, their location, their resources, and their philosophies or missions. Although space does not permit such an exercise, it raises one final issue, the transportabliity of counseling theory and practice across national boundaries.

Transportability of Counseling Theory and Practice Across National Boundaries

If there are national differences in the provision of counseling services and in their shape and substance, the next question is to what degree can models of counseling theory and practice be adopted and implemented across national boundaries? There is, in fact, no answer to the question. There are indications, however, that cultural limits have an impact on the adoption of counseling models.

Bergin (1985), for example, indicated that psychotherapy as we know it has been formulated mainly in the secular centers of Western Europe and North America. Therefore, there is a cultural narrowness about values and mental health that can be expected to impede the assimilations of psychotherapy into non-Western nations. As Reynolds (1980), among others, reported, Western therapies have a particular way of looking at and processing human behavior; Eastern therapies have a different way of defining such behavior and planning interventions. One is not necessarily a substitute for the other because value sets, assumptions, and cultural artifacts make some forms of counseling and psychotherapy unacceptable or ineffective in cultures different from those in which such interventions were invented. An interesting example is the lack of adherents to psychoanalytic therapy in Japan, in contrast to the rather wide acceptance of such a treatment approach in Western Europe and the United States. The difference does not seem to lie in economics; the contemporary Japanese, like his or her Western counterpart, is able to afford the cost (DeVos, 1980). The issue lies elsewhere, most likely in values, structuring of emotions, and perceptions of interpersonal relationships.

Psychoanalytic theory tends to value such behavior as self-consciousness and independence from parents as prized therapeutic outcomes. Confucianism, the code of Bushido, Zen Buddhism, and other philosophical or cultural guides to Japanese behavior do not value independence or individualism. Rather they value loyalty to others, gratitude to others, self-discipline, conformity, group identity, and interpersonal support as mature, and, therefore, as therapeutic outcomes. Delving into the unconscious may threaten family cohesion, thus the psychotherapies valued in Japan are those, whether Western or Eastern in origin, that accommodate and promote such values as family unity and respect. Beyond this, Japanese psychology is not one of analysis, causality, rationality, and linear logic. It is instead one of metaphor, allusion, nuance, and syncretic thinking. Unlike Westerners who reject psychoanalytic thought because of its emphasis on the irrational, even primordial, character of much of human behavior, the Japanese reject it because the value sets of individuality, autonomy, and self-awareness are inconsistent with those of social integration and family unity and responsibility.

Another example of value differences between East and West is a Taiwanese-American comparison (Saner-Yiu & Saner, 1985). This work suggests the characteristics of value conflicts between cultures or nations that revolve around whether the nations are essentially individualistic or collectivist in their psychology. The authors believe that cultural values are non-negotiable structural elements of human existence that influence perception, cognition, and behavior. "Different cultures engender different cognitive coping processes, which in turn influence the way people experience and live reality" (p. 139).

In essence, Saner-Yiu and Saner (1985) contended that the value assumptions embedded in counseling approaches derived from an individualist culture (e.g., the United States) are in conflict in their adoption by a collectivist nation (e.g., Taiwan). Assumptions about self-disclosure, right to private life and opinion, "I" consciousness, individual initiative and achievement, interpersonal relationships, and related cultural dimensions are not shared across nations, particularly those classified as Eastern in their culture and philosophy (Okon, 1983; Shanhirzadi, 1983). It is equally likely that differences in "world view" as defined by culturally determined value sets exist between the nations of the Northern and Southern hemisphere, and between the industrialized and non-industrialized nations. Therefore, value conflicts become major ingredients in the assimilation and adaptation of counseling theory and practice across national boundaries, and shed significant doubt about the utility or the reality of cross-cultural accommodation of theory and practice without significant analysis of the value sets implied.

CONCLUSION

In addition to acknowledging that values issues exist at every level within the counseling process, this article has attempted to explore ways in which values can interact with a variety of counseling variables (i.e., counselor-client, counselor-client-counseling strategy, counseling strategy-national differences) to either facilitate or impede the therapeutic process. To this end, it has been noted that a lack of explicitness with regard to the values assumed by counselors, counseling approaches, and intervention strategies can result in tensions between counselors and clients, counselors and institutions, or specific models of counseling and their acceptance in individual nations.

To avoid cultural encapsulation, counselors need to be sensitive to the assumptions underlying the values held by counselors, clients, and counseling models, as well as the values being propagated at the national level at any point in time. Beyond this, counselors need to gain an awareness of the possible permutations and combinations that can occur as client, counselor, counseling strategy, and national differences interact.

REFERENCES

Anastasi, A. (1982). *Psychological testing* (5th ed.). New York: Macmillan.

Bergin, A. E. (1985). Proposed values for guiding and evaluating counseling and psychotherapy. *Counseling and Values, 29,* 99–115.

Buss, A. H. (1966). *Psychopathology.* New York: Wiley and Sons.

Butcher, J. N., & Pancheria, P. (1976). *A handbook of cross-national MMPI research.* Minneapolis, MN: University of Minnesota Press.

DeVos, G. (1980). Afterword. In D. K. Reynolds (Ed.), *The quiet therapies: Japanese pathways to personal growth* (pp. 113–132). Honolulu: The University Press of Hawaii.

Herr, E. L. (1982). Perspectives of the philosophical, empirical, and cost-benefit effects of guidance and counseling: Implications for political action. *Personnel and Guidance Journal, 60,* 594–597.

Hofstede, G. (1984). *Culture's consequences.* Beverly Hills, CA: Sage.

Kluckhohn C. (1951). Values and value orientations in the theory of action. In T. Parsons & E. A. Shields (Eds.), *Toward a general theory of action* (pp. 388–433)). Cambridge, MA: Harvard University Press.

Kluckhohn, C. (1956). Toward a comparison of value-emphases in different cultures. In L. D. White (Ed.), *The state of social sciences* (pp. 116–132). Chicago: University of Chicago Press.

Kluckhohn, F. R., & Stodtbeck, F. L. (1961). *Variations in value orientations.* Evanston, IL: Row, Peterson.

London, P. (1964). *The modes and morals of psychotherapy.* New York: Holt, Rinehart, and Winston.

Marsella, A. J., & Pedersen, P. (Eds.). (1981). *Cross-cultural counseling and psychotherapy: Foundations, evaluation, and ethnocultural considerations.* Elmsford, NY: Pergamon.

Okon, S. E. (1983). Guidance and counseling services in Nigeria. *Personnel and Guidance Journal, 61,* 457–459.

Padilla, A. M., Ruiz, R. A., & Alvarez, R. (1975). Community mental health service for the Spanish-speaking/surnamed population. *American Psychologist, 30,* 892–905.

Peterson, J. A. (1985). The counselor and change: Counseling for cultural transition. *Counseling and Values, 29,* 117–127.

Phenix, P. H. (1973, March). *Basic value issues in career education for the gifted and talented.* Paper presented at the First National Seminar on Career Education for Gifted and Talented Students, University of Maryland.

Pietrofesa, J. J., Hoffman, A., Splete, H., & Pinto, D. (1978). *Counseling: Theory, research, and practice.* Chicago: Rand McNally.

Pine, G. J. (1972). Counseling minority groups: A review of the literature. *Counseling and Values, 17,* 35–44.

Reynolds, D. K. (1980). *The quite therapies: Japanese pathways to personal growth.* Honolulu: The University Press of Hawaii.

Roberts, K. (1981). The sociology of work entry and occupational choice. In A. G. Watts, D. E. Super, & J. M. Kidd (Eds.), *Career development in Britain* (pp. 279–299). Cambridge, England: Hobson's Press Limited.

Rogers, C. R. (1951). *Client-centered therapy: Its current practice, implications and theory*. Boston: Houghton Mifflin.

Saner-Yiu, L., & Saner, R. (1985). Value dimensions in American counseling: A Taiwanese-American comparison. *International Journal for the Advancement of Counseling, 8*, 137–146.

Schofield, W. (1964). *Psychotherapy: The purchase of friendship*. Englewood Cliffs, NJ: Prentice-Hall.

Shanhirzadi, A. (1983). Counseling Iranians. *Personnel and Guidance Journal, 51*, 487–489.

Sue, D. W. (1981). *Counseling the culturally different: Theory and practice*. New York: John Wiley and Sons.

Sue, D. W. (1977). Counseling the culturally different: A conceptual analysis. *Personnel and Guidance Journal, 55*, 422–425.

Sue, S. (1983). Ethnic minority issues in psychology: A reexamination. *American Psychologist, 38*, 583–592.

Super, D. E. (1983). Synthesis: Or is it distillation? *Personnel and Guidance Journal, 61*, 511–514.

Swanson, G. (1972). Philosophical bases for career education. In J. Maigisos (Ed.), *Career education* (pp. 40–49). Washington, DC: American Vocational Association.

Vaisey, J., & Clark, C. F. O. (1976). *Education: The state of the debate in America, Britain, and Canada*. London, England: Gerald Duckworth and Company, Limited.

Walters. O. S. (1958). Metaphysics, religion, and psychotherapy. *Journal of Counseling Psychology, 5*, 243–252.

Watts, A. G., & Herr, E. L. (1976). Career(s) education in Britain and the USA: Contrasts and common problems. *British Journal of Guidance and Counseling, 4*(2), 129–142.

Wrenn, C. G. (1962). The culturally encapsulated counselor. *Harvard Educational Review, 32*, 444–449.

Values in Counseling and Psychotherapy

C. H. PATTERSON

VALUES ARE DIFFICULT TO DEFINE even though everyone recognizes and uses the concept. The failure of writers to define values or attempt to delineate the nature of the concept has led to some confusion and fuzziness in discussions in the literature.

Kluckhohn, an anthropologist, noted that the concept of values involves the concept of "the desirable, which influences the selection, from available modes, means, and ends of action.... Value implies a code or standard, which has some persistence through time, or put more broadly, which organizes a system of action. Values, conveniently and in accord with received usage, place things, acts, ways of behaving, goals of action, on the approval-disapproval continuum" (Kluckhohn, et al., p. 395). But values carry more than an approval-disapproval connotation. Smith's (1954) definition is more accurate. He stated that "by values, I shall mean a person's implicit or explicit standards of choice, insofar as these are invested with obligation or requiredness" (p. 513). The words *society's* and *culture's* should to added to *person's* in the definition. It makes clear the *oughtness* or *should* nature of values. Thus, it avoids the frequent confusion of values with preferences—tastes, likes, and interests. The objects of such preferences may be said to be valued, but they do not constitute values. There is no *obligatoriness* or *requiredness* attached to them.

The relationship, or difference, between values and morals is not always clear. It seems that morals are a class of values, specifically relating to interpersonal relations. Grant (1985) noted that "moral values are distinguished from values in general in that they encompass only attitudes towards other individuals and attitudes towards actions that affect them" (p. 143). Thus, morals are more specific than values. This article is concerned with values in a broader sense, even though the counselor's or therapist's attitudes toward the client that are implemented in the therapy relationship may be considered moral values, and even though the values represented in other aspects of therapy may have moral implications (cf. Grant, 1985).

Preferences vary widely among individuals and societies or cultures, but there are some values that seem to be universal. "Thou shalt not kill" is, perhaps, the most widely recognized and accepted value. Honesty, the obligation to tell the truth, is another widely accepted value. Freedom is, perhaps, a third. These values seem to be based on requirements necessary for the survival of society. A society whose members kill each other will not survive. Neither will a society in which a basic minimum of honesty and truthfulness is not present. (At one time, some primitive societies that were organized on the basis of deceit may have existed, but they have not persisted.) History seems to indicate the prevalence of the value of freedom, as evidenced by resistance and revolution when freedom is restricted or denied.

Certain values are universal, but this does not mean that they are absolute. Killing may be permitted in certain circumstances—to get rid of a tyrant to obtain freedom, to execute a heinous criminal, to preserve one's life, or in war, to preserve the society. Lying may be permitted—to save a life, to mislead the enemy during wartime, to spare a terminally ill patient from further worry in certain cases, or to prevent a child from getting hurt in specific circumstances. But in each case, it is recognized as an exception to be justified, usually in terms of another value taking precedence. Some values are not absolute, but this does not mean that they are relative, except in the sense that they are relative to each other.

There are other lower order, limited values, or values that are elements of, or related to, more universal or higher values. One must be careful, however, that preferences or tastes are not elevated to the level of values and then propagated as desirable for all persons. There are several ways in which values are involved in counseling or psychotherapy.

CLIENT VALUES IN PSYCHOTHERAPY

There seems to be little, if any, disagreement that the counselor deals with value problems and issues brought to counseling by the client. The counselor need not accept or approve of the client's values. Disagreement with or nonacceptance of the client's values does not mean that the client is not accepted as a person. The way in which the client's values and value problems are dealt with does, however, constitute an issue in counseling. This process will be discussed in the following sections.

THE COUNSELOR'S VALUES IN PSYCHOTHERAPY

During the first half of this century, the position taken on the counselor's values in counseling or psychotherapy was that of orthodox psychoanalysis. The analyst, it was presumed, functioned as a blank screen upon which the client projected his or her beliefs, attitudes, and values. The therapist was neutral; his or her values were not involved.

COUNSELOR IMPOSITION OF VALUES

Associated with the orthodox psychoanalytic view was the belief that the analyst ought to remain neutral. Wilder, commenting on an article by

Ginsberg and Herma (1953), noted that "it has been taken for granted that the analyst must not try to impose his [or her] value systems on the patient." Deutsch and Murphy (1955) stated that "the therapist should by all means avoid impressing his [or her] own philosophy on a patient" (p. 8). Although this position seems to be the prevailing one and counseling students are usually admonished not to impose their values or value system on clients, this position is not universally accepted. Wilder (Ginsberg & Herma, 1953) referred to "rising voices to the effect that the analyst not only does but should transmit his [or her] value system to the patient." He continued, "A patient often says, 'Doctor, after all, you seem to have found a measure of peace and stability; why don't you shorten therapy by simply telling me your philosophy?' " Weisskopf-Joelson (1953) proposed that the inculcation of a philosophy of life should be considered as one of the objectives of psychotherapy. Beutler (1979), viewing psychotherapy as a process of persuasion, seems to "consider the therapy process as one which systematically induces the patient to develop alternative beliefs which approximate *those of the therapist*" (p. 432).

Some years ago, Murphy (1955), writing to counselors, asked, "Shall personnel and guidance work . . . attempt to impart a philosophy of life?" Although Murphy conceded that "no one knows enough to construct an adequate philosophy of life," he wrote that "nevertheless if he who offers guidance is a whole person, with real roots in human culture, he cannot help conveying directly or indirectly to every client what he himself sees and feels, and the perspective in which his own life is lived." He suggested that "it is not true that the wise man's sharing of a philosophy of life is an arrogant imposition upon a defenseless client." He felt that the young need help and advice from those who have thought things through. But he warned counselors not to "attempt the arrogant and self-defeating task of guiding men and women without a rich, flexible, and ever-growing system of values of your own" (p. 8).

Wrenn (1958) less strongly wrote that the counselor "may or may not . . . assist the client in an understanding of life's purposes and meanings, and the alternate ways in which one may related oneself to the Infinite" (p. 332). Counselors with a religious orientation seem to be more accepting of the appropriateness of directly influencing client values than are counselors without a strong religious orientation. But direct influence of client values and philosophy is not limited to counselors with a religious commitment. Several theorists support such an approach. Williamson's approach (Patterson, 1980) involves direct instruction. Ellis's rational-emotive therapy (Patterson, 1986) is, essentially, instruction in a philosophy of life. Victor Frankl (Patterson, 1986) also instructs clients in values and in an approach to living. In addition, Thorne, (Patterson, 1986) included reeducation in a philosophy of life as a method of counseling.

There are several reasons why it might be inappropriate for a counselor or therapist to indoctrinate clients or attempt to inculcate a system of values or a philosophy of life in them.

1. Though there are, no doubt, some generally and even universally accepted values, principles, or ethical standards, these do not constitute a philosophy of life. Each individual's philosophy is unique in some details, although it may have much in common with the philosophies of others, particularly those in the same culture. No individual's philosophy is necessarily appropriate for another individual. Yet, a philosophy that does not include the basic universal values is not an acceptable or viable philosophy for existence in a society.

2. It is too much to expect all counselors or psychotherapists to have a fully developed, adequate, or ideal philosophy of life ready to be impressed on clients. Murphy, quoted above (1955), referred to a wise man's sharing of a philosophy of life. But sharing is one thing, and instructing or guiding is another. Moreover, not all counselors are "wise men."

3. It may be questioned whether the counseling or therapy relationship is the appropriate place for instruction in ethics and a philosophy of life. Among many, there is an apparent confusion between counseling and tutoring or individual instruction. The home, the church, and the school are appropriate places for such instruction.

4. An individual usually does not adopt a system or code of ethics or a philosophy of life from one source at a particular time. (Religious conversion is an exception.) These are products of many influences over a long period of time.

5. It would seem to be best for each individual to develop his or her own unique philosophy of life from many sources and not to be deprived of the experience of doing so. Such a philosophy will probably be more useful and meaningful than one adopted ready-made from someone else, no matter how wise such a person may be. A viable philosophy cannot be impressed from outside of oneself but must be developed from within.

6. Finally, the imposition of values or a philosophy on clients is inconsistent with the values of some systems of psychotherapy. These systems accept the right of the client to refuse to accept or develop any system of values or ethics, and to endure the consequences of such choices.

The counselor or therapist should not impose his or her values on clients, but this does not mean that the therapist should refuse to discuss values, ethics, or philosophy. Nor does it mean that the therapist may not, at times, express his or her values. The therapist may do so at the request of the client. In addition, there may be times when the therapist thinks it is necessary or desirable for the client to be aware of these values, or times in which the client should know how the therapist stands on certain ethical or value issues. Being genuine or honest in the relationship sometimes means that the therapist should express his or her values. When therapists believe that the therapy relationship or process would be improved by explicitly acknowledging their values and beliefs, they can do so. Such values should be clearly labeled as their own (or possibly sometimes as society's in general). When values are openly expressed in this way, there is no coerciveness about them. In addition to the explicit imposition of the counselor's values in psychotherapy, there are several other ways in which the counselor's values enter the process of counseling or psychotherapy.

IMPLICIT INVOLVEMENT OF COUNSELOR VALUES

The problem is not simply whether or not therapists should openly impose their values on clients. Can therapists avoid influencing the values of their clients?

The attempt to define psychotherapy as a science or a technology would seem to remove values from the process (Margolis, 1966). Many years ago Watson (1958) wrote that "one of the falsehoods with which some therapists console themselves is that their form of treatment is purely technical, so they need take no stand on moral issues" (p. 575). More recently, Garfield and Bergin (1986) noted that "progress is developing new and more effective techniques of psychotherapy" has obscured "the fact that subjective value decisions underlie the choice of techniques, the goals of change, and the assessment of what is a 'good' outcome" (p. 16).

Many psychoanalysts came to realize that the therapist could not remain a neutral figure to the client. The effort to remain a "blank screen" was intended to allow the client to project his or her perceptions on the therapist—the creation of a transference. But the analyst was not, in fact, a blank screen, and the "real person" of the therapist was involved in the relationship. As Wolberg noted (comment in Ginsburg & Herma, 1953):

> No matter how passive the therapist may believe himself [or herself] to be, and no matter how objective he [or she] remains in an attempt to allow the patient to develop his [or her] own sense of values, there is an inevitable incorporation within the patient of a new superego patterned after the character of the therapist as he [or she] is perceived by the patient. There is almost inevitably an acceptance by the patient of many of the values of the therapist as they are communicated in the interpretation or through direct suggestion, or as they are deduced by the patient from his [or her] association with the therapist.

Karl Menninger (1958) wrote the following:

> We cannot ignore the fact that what the psychoanalyst believes, what he [or she] lives for, what he [or she] considers to be the purpose of life and the joy of life, what he [or she] considers to be the purpose of life and the joy of life, what he [or she] considers to be good and what he [or she] consider to be evil, become known to the patient and influence him [or her] enormously, not as "suggestion" but as inspiration. . . . No matter how skillful the analyst in certain technical maneuvers, his [or her] ultimate product, like Galatea, will reflect not only his [or her] handicraft but his [or her] character. (p. 91)

And Ingham and Love (1954) wrote the following:

> The existence of the therapeutic relationship puts the therapist in a position in which he [or she] does, without choice, influence values in the mind of the patient. It is almost impossible for the therapist to avoid giving some impression of whether he [or she] favors such thing as general law and order, personal self-development, and emotional maturity. . . . If they have discussed an issue that involves moral values for a period of time, it is evident that the patient will have a concept of what the therapist thinks. His [or her] attitudes about right and wrong, or good and bad, are likely to be particularly influential for the patient. (pp. 75–76)

Because clients perceive the values of therapists' as well as their interests and beliefs, even when these are not overtly expressed, clients focus on different things with different therapists or with therapists who operate from particular theoretical orientations. When therapists value dreams, clients dream and report their dreams; when therapists value sexual material or any other specific content material, clients produce it, thus "validating" the theories of their therapists.

Several research studies provide evidence for the therapist's influence on client values, beginning with an early study by Rosenthal (1955). (See Beutler [1979] for other references.)

The recognition that the values of the counselor or therapist cannot be kept out of the therapy relationship makes it imperative that counselors be clearly aware of their values, and clear about how these values are and should be involved in their counseling. The current emphasis on techniques in therapy, and on skill training in the education of counselors, clouds this recognition. The concept of the therapist as a technician is kept to a minimum if it includes the consideration of the therapist's values. The awareness that the therapist is a person who is participating in a personal relationship with the client brings the importance of the therapist's values into focus.

VALUES IN COUNSELING PHILOSOPHY AND THEORY

Values, as Glad (1959) noted, are inherent in theories of counseling or psychotherapy. It is likely that students and therapists select a theoretical orientation (to the extent that they are aware of theories and are theory oriented) on the basis of the congruence of the philosophy and values of the theory with their own values and philosophy. Although most, if not all, theories profess to respect the autonomy of the client, there is considerable variation in the degree to which this respect is manifested. Some years ago, I suggested that there were two contrasting approaches to human relations, including psychotherapy (Patterson, 1958, 1959). One, labeled the manipulative or authoritarian approach, emphasized the authority, prestige, status, and expertise of the therapist. The other, labeled the understanding approach, emphasized empathic understanding, warmth, respect, and genuineness. Theories or approaches to counseling or psychotherapy can be roughly classified into these two categories, representing quite contrasting philosophies and values. Current support for this classification comes from the 1985 Phoenix conference on the Evaluation of Psychotherapy, at which 7,000 people from 29 countries gathered to hear the world's greatest living therapists or theorists. Margo Adler (incidentally, a granddaughter of Alfred Adler) reported on the conference for the National Public Radio program, *All Things Considered*. There were two kinds of therapists at the conference, she said—the manipulators and the enablers, or facilitators, and she illustrated the differences with quotations from speakers.

These two orientations represent two different value systems and two different views of clients. They have implications for the goals and methods of psychotherapy.

The Therapist's Goals as Values

"Both the therapist's goals and the methods selected to achieve them can be viewed as reflecting distinct value orientations" (Madell, 1982, p. 52). A review of the many and varied goals of psychotherapy is not possible here. In an edited volume 20 years ago, (Mahrer, 1967) revealed the wide variety of goals advocated by various therapists. Taking a cue from Parloff (1967), I have organized goals into three levels: ultimate, mediate, and immediate (Patterson, 1970, 1985). The *ultimate goal* is a broad, general goal, incorporating many of the concepts of various theories and philosophies of therapy, and it represents an ideal. It is an attempt to answer the following questions: What do we want our clients to be like? What should people be like? What kind of person do we want or need in a desirable world? This involves the goal of life or living together as human beings. The term or concept that can incorporate this goal is self-acutalization, as defined by the work of Maslow (1956). Rogers's concept of the fully functioning person is similar (Rogers, 1969). It is unfortunate that the concept of self-actualization has been misunderstood and misrepresented by several writers, including some prominent psychologists (Patterson, 1985). It has been presented as self-centered, selfish, antisocial, represented in the "me generation" of the 1960s and in some of the activities of the human potential movement. But, in Maslow's description, it includes an acceptance of and empathy for others. Rogers's descriptions include concern for others; the self-actualizing person must live in a society of others (Rogers, 1959, 1969).

Self-actualization—or the self-actualizing process—is a goal common to all persons. As adequately defined, it is a goal that is not limited by time or culture. It might be considered the highest value for human beings. It is a goal that is not limited to psychotherapy—it is, or should be, the goal of society and of all its institutions. It is a goal that is not chosen by the therapist or the client, nor is it simply a religious or philosophical goal. It is derived from the nature of the human being, indeed, of all living organisms, whose nature is the actualization of potentials. The actualization of potentials is the basic, dominant nature of life. This derivation of a value from the nature of living organisms can be criticized for being what philosophers call the Natural Fallacy (Margolis, 1966). But it seems only reasonable that values may be evaluated in terms of their relation to (supportive of or in disagreement with) the nature of human beings and their developments. Skinner (1953) suggested that science can provide a basis for values:

> If a science of behavior can discover those conditions of life [that] make for the strength of men, it may provide a set of "moral values" which, because they are independent of the history and culture of any one group, may be generally adopted. (p. 445)

It can be maintained that the ultimate "strength of men" lies in the characteristics of self-actualizing persons, and unless there are enough individuals possessing the characteristics to a minimal degree, society cannot survive. Historically, self-actualizing men and women have been the major contributors to the development of civilization.

Therapists who disclaim any ultimate goal may, nevertheless, implicitly have such a goal and impose this goal on their clients while being unaware that they are doing so. The reluctance of counselors or therapists to adopt an ultimate goal is based on the difficulties of defining such a goal (such as "mental health," for example). But self-actualization, properly defined is a goal that more and more psychologists and psychotherapists are adopting, in one form or another or under one rubric or another.

The *mediate goals* of counseling or therapy are the more specific goals that are usually the concern of counselors. Although the ultimate goal is common to all persons, mediate goals vary with individuals. They include such things as educational and career goals, family and personal relationships, and the common objectives of symptom removal or alleviation, reduction of psychological pain and suffering. These goals may be related to the ultimate goal in two ways: They are steps or means toward becoming a more self-actualizing person, or they may be by-products of the development of the more abstract qualities of becoming a more self-actualizing person. Besides integrating common and individual goals, the concept of an ultimate goal provides a criterion for the acceptability of individual goals. In addition, while the ultimate goal is, in effect, a given and is not chosen by either the therapist or the client, mediate goals are chosen by the client.

The *immediate goal* of counseling or psychotherapy is the initiation and continuation of the process of counseling or psychotherapy, the process by which the client achieves mediate goals and becomes a more self-actualizing person. The methods or techniques are chosen by the counselor or therapist. They represent the values of the therapist. They will differ radically depending on whether the therapist functions as a facilitator or enabler, or as a director or manipulator. The therapist as a facilitator is consistent with the ultimate goal of self-actualization. The self-actualizing person is autonomous, independent, and responsible (responsibly independent). The therapist's methods are consistent with these characteristics, providing a relationship in which the client is respected and given responsibility in and for the therapy process and is expected to make choices and decisions. These methods are presented in what Strupp (1980) referred to as *essential* therapeutic values: "People have the right to personal freedom and independence;" as members of society, "they have rights and privileges" and also "responsibilities to others;" they should, "to the greatest extent possible, be responsible for conducting their own affairs;" "their individuality should be fully respected, and they should not be controlled, dominated, manipulated, coerced or indoctrinated;" "people are entitled to make their own mistakes and to learn from their own life experiences" (pp. 397–398).

The essential condition for such a process is a relationship characterized by empathic understanding; respect, warmth or caring; and genuineness or honesty.

The Therapist's Communication of Values

The therapist's values are, as Strupp noted, not communicated directly to the client. Yet, they *are* communicated in the following ways:

1. The methods the therapist uses, as noted, represent values. They communicate the essential therapeutic values listed above, or the lack of them.
2. The therapist's methods are not simply objective techniques but are part of the therapist as a person. The therapist as a person relates to the client as a person. The therapist becomes a model for the client. As the therapist shows empathic understanding, respect, and genuineness in a positive relationship, the client also becomes more empathic, respecting of others, and genuine.
3. The responses of the therapist reveal what the therapist values—they reinforce certain behaviors in the client. In these behaviors, the client proceeds from self-disclosure to the specific content of self-exploration. These responses also reveal whether the therapist considers himself or herself an expert by leading, questioning, interpreting, guiding, suggesting, advising, or whether the therapist places the responsibility on the client by listening, responding, and following the client.

A DILEMMA AND ITS RESOLUTION

The therapist, it has been emphasized, should not impose his or her value beliefs, value system, or philosophy on clients. Yet, it has also been noted, the therapist cannot avoid communicating his or her values to the client through the acceptance of an ultimate goal—the kind of behavior or person toward which therapy is directed—and through the methods or procedures used to implement the therapeutic process. Thus, there is a conflict or dilemma. The ultimate goal requires freedom and autonomy for the client, yet the client does not choose the goal or methods, nor can he or she avoid being exposed to and influenced by the procedures of the therapist. The methods of the therapist, however, must be consistent with the ultimate goal of the therapy. (And this goal, although in a sense "imposed" by the therapist, is not actually imposed because it is derived from the nature of the client and human beings—it is imposed by this nature). These conditions lead to the goal of a self-actualizing person. As Rogers (1961) phrased it:

> ... We have established by external control conditions which we predict will be followed by internal control by the individual, in pursuit of internally chosen goals . . . the client will become more self-directing, less rigid, more open to the evidence of his [or her] senses, better organized and integrated, more similar to the ideal he [or she] has chosen for himself [or herself]. (p. 397)

In other words, the client becomes more self-actualizing.

A POSTSCRIPT

There is a recent development that could have a significant effect on the relation of values to psychotherapy—in effect, "devaluing" psychotherapy. This is the attempt to "medicalize" psychotherapy. About two decades ago, the medical model of psychotherapy was rejected by clinical psychologists. More recently, however, it has been re-espoused. The basic reason for this is that if psychotherapy is to be covered by insurance, it must be a treatment for a medical condition—and, perhaps, could not be expected to—cover a social-psychological disorder—a problem in living. In addition to the threat to independent practitioners of psychotherapy by nonmedical therapists, there are other implications for the practice of psychotherapy and research. The medical model involves specific treatments for specific conditions. Insurers as well as "clinicians and policy makers need to know the extent to which treatments achieve desired or optimal therapeutic outcomes with the least restrictive and costly effort" (Newman & Howard, 1986, p. 181; see also Howard, Kapka, Krause, & Orlinsky; 1986; Kisch & Kroll, 1980). This has led to attempts by some psychologists and psychiatrists to standardize treatment, to the extent of developing manuals that therapists are to follow. "The proliferation of manuals for treating particular ills by particular methods reflects the confidence of increased rigor in controlled research and increasing acceptance of brief clinical psychotherapies" (Parloff, London, & Wolfe, 1986 p. 337–338). Although this seems to be desirable for controlled research, there is a question as to whether this should, or even can, be done. Goldfried (1982) wrote:

> Should psychotherapy be made more scientific? Can psychotherapy be made more scientific, i.e., can its activities be made more measurable and replicable? . . . The rigorous research design does not place sufficient value on the centrality of the therapeutic alli-

ance—the depth, stability, and benignity of the relationship between therapist and patient. . . . Can a psychological intervention ever be as fully specified and be made a "pure" as a pharmacological one? (pp. 342–343)

Beyond this, the implications for values and ethical problems in psychotherapy are radical. At one extreme, clients with problems involving values, choices, and issues involved in living would not be eligible for or entitled to psychotherapy—because, indeed, they are not eligible now for insured treatment without a diagnosis of psychopathology. Goals and methods of treatment would be prescribed with the therapist having no choices to make, no value decisions. He or she would be simply a technician following a manual. The relationship would not be important, let alone the essence of psychotherapy. This would dispose of the value problems in psychotherapy; it would also dispose of psychotherapy.

CONCLUSION

Beutler, Crago, and Arizmendi (1986) recently noted that "many authors are urging therapists both to attend to their own religious and attitudinal systems and to be aware of the potential value of those of their patients" (p. 274). It is interesting that this comment is in the present tense, suggesting that it is only recently that the importance of values in psychotherapy has been recognized. Yet, the citations in this article (and they are by no means complete) go back some 35 years. With the exception of discussions of cross-cultural psychotherapy, few textbooks give much consideration to the place of values in counseling and psychotherapy. Yet, the problem of values permeates the entire process, entering into the goals and methods of every theory or approach. In this article, I have presented and considered the issues and have suggested an approach to counseling and psychotherapy that recognizes and incorporates those values that are basic to a democratic philosophy and the goal of a democratic society—the development of self-actualizing persons.

REFERENCES

Beutler, L. E. (1979). Values, beliefs, religion and the persuasive influence of psychotherapy. *Psychotherapy: Theory, Research and Practice, 16,* 432–440.

Beutler, L. E., Crago, M., & Arizmendi, T. G. (1986). Research on therapist variables in psychotherapy. In S. L. Garfield and A. E. Bergin (Eds.), *Handbook of psychotherapy and behavior change* (pp. 257–310). New York: Wiley.

Deutsch, F., & Murphy, W. F. (1955). *The clinical interview.* New York: International Universities Press.

Garfield, S. L., & Bergin, A. E. (1986). Introduction and historical overview. In S. L. Garfield & A. E. Bergin (Eds.), *Handbook of psychotherapy and behavior change* (pp. 3–22). New York: Wiley.

Ginsberg, W. W., & Herma, J. L. (1953). Values and their relationship to psychiatric principles and practice. *American Journal of Psychotherapy, 7,* 536—573.

Glad, D. D. (1959). *Operational values in psychotherapy*. Ne York: Oxford University Press.

Goldfried, M.R. (1982). *Converging themes in psychotherapy: Trends in psychodynamic, humanistic, and behavioral practice*. New York: Springer.

Grant, B. (1985). The moral nature of psychotherapy. *Counseling and Values, 29*, 141–150.

Howard, K. I., Kapka, S. M., Krause, M. S., & Orlinsky, D. E. (1986). The dose-effect relationship in psychotherapy. *American Psychologist, 41*, 159–164.

Ingham, H.V., & Love, O.R. (1954). *The process of psychotherapy*. New York: McGraw-Hill.

Kisch, J., & Kroll, J. (1980). Meaningfulness versus effectiveness: Paradoxical implication in the evaluation of psychotherapy. *Psychotherapy: Theory, Research and Practice, 17*, 401–413.

Kluckhohn, C., et al. (1952). Values and value orientation in the theory of action. In T. Parsons & E. A. Shils (Eds.), *Toward a general theory of action* (pp. 288–443). Cambridge, MA: Harvard University Press.

Madell, T. O. (1982). The relationship between values and attitudes toward three therapy methods. *Counseling and Values, 27*, 52–60.

Mahrer, A. R. (1967). *The goals of psychotherapy*. New York: Appleton-Century-Crofts (Prentice-Hall).

Margolis, J. (1966). *Psychotherapy and mortality: A study of two concepts*. New York: Random House.

Maslow, A. H. (1957). Self-actualizing people: A study of psychological health. In C. E. Monstakas (Ed.), *The self: Explorations in personal growth* (pp. 160–194). New York: Harper & Row.

Menninger, K. (1958). *Theory of psychoanalytic technique*. New York: Basic Books.

Murphy, G. (1955). The cultured context of guidance. *Personnel and Guidance Journal, 34*, 4–9.

Newman, F. L., & Howard, K. (1986). Therapeutic effect, treatment outcome, and national health policy. *American Psychologist, 41*, 181–187.

Parloff, N. B. (1967). Goals in psychotherapy: Mediating and ultimate. In A. R. Mahrer (Ed.), *The goals of psychotherapy* (pp. 5–19). New York: Appleton-Century-Crofts (Prentice-Hall).

Parloff, M. B., London, P., & Wolfe, B. (1986). Individual psychotherapy and behavior change. *Annual Review of Psychology, 37*, 321–349.

Patterson, C. H. (1958). Two approaches to human relations. *American Journal of Psychotherapy, 12*, 691–708.

Patterson, C. H. (1959). *Counseling and psychotherapy: Theory and practice*. New York: Harper & Row.

Patterson, C. H. (1970). A model for counseling and other interpersonal relationships. In W. H. Van Hoose & J. J. Pietrofesa (Eds.), *Counseling and guidance in the twentieth century* (pp. 169–190). Boston: Houghton Mifflin.

Patterson, C. H. (1980). *Theories of counseling and psychotherapy*. (3rd ed.). New York: Harper & Row).

Patterson, C. H. (1985). *The therapeutic relationship: Foundations for an eclectic psychotherapy*. Monterey, CA: Brooks/Cole.

Patterson, C. H. (1986). *Theories of counseling and psychotherapy*. (4th ed.). New York: Harper & Row.

Rosenthal, D. (1955). Changes in some values following psychotherapy. *Journal of Consulting Psychology, 19*, 431–436.

Rogers, C. R. (1959). A theory of therapy, personality and interpersonal relationship, as developed in the client-centered framework. In S. Koch (Ed.), *Psychology: A study of science*. (Vol. 3, pp. 184–256). New York: McGraw-Hill.

Rogers, C. R. (1961). *On becoming a person*. Boston: Houghton Mifflin.

Rogers, C. R. (1969). *Freedom to learn*. Columbus, OH: Merrill.

Skinner, B. F. (1953). *Science and human behavior*. New York: Macmillan.

Smith, M. B. (1954). Toward scientific and professional responsibility. *American Psychologist, 9,* 513–516.

Strupp, H. H. (1980). Humanism and psychotherapy: A personal statement of the therapist's essential values. *Psychotherapy: Theory, Research and Practice, 17,* 396–400.

Watson, G. (1958). Moral issues in psychotherapy. *American Psychologist, 13,* 574–576.

Weisskopf-Joelson, E. (1953). Some suggestions concerning Weltanschauung and psychotherapy. *Journal of Abnormal and Social Psychology, 48,* 601–604.

Wrenn, C. G., (1958). Psychology, religion, and values for the counselor. *Personnel and Guidance Journal, 36,* 331–334.

Counseling the Culturally Different

C. JERRY DOWNING

FOR YEARS, COUNSELORS have struggled with a variety of approaches related to counseling the culturally different. This article is intended to address those issues from the position that everyone is culturally different. From this theoretical position, it is relatively easy to develop a model of counseling to serve all people. The model, though not difficult to develop, does demand a highly flexible counselor value system. Students in counselor education classes and counselors in the field have found this position appealing since it allows them to be effective helpers to everyone.

As the reader may suspect, one problem arises very early with this approach in terms of counselor values. If services are offered to all people, the counselor must be prepared to treat all clients with some degree of equality. Therefore, counselors must be acutely aware of their own values and prejudices. But, what else is new? The new for counselor self-awareness is of equal importance whether the client is a Native American or a hysterical type. At issue is the determination of a theoretical orientation that allows the counselor to confront internal value conflicts regardless of the culture of the client. In some respects, it may be easier to be aware of bias when the client is distinctly culturally different. If the client looks and dresses similar to the counselor, it might be logical to assume a similarity in thought and values as well. It is with this problem that the values clarification process provides an essential counselor education function.

The second major demand of this approach involves data gathering. If the counselor assumes that everyone is culturally different, then a primary counseling behavior must be that of learning about the individual's culture. The data-gathering process will likely be as individual as are the cultures to be explored. The system by which a counselor learns about a person's culture must be acceptable to the individual client, and counselors need to be particularly sensitive to individual cultural differences as they gather data. Again, the values clarification process aids in developing and maintaining an appropriate level of sensitivity to the needs of others (Simon, Howe, & Kirschenbaum, 1972). In the very few years that counselors have seriously considered the issues of counseling the culturally different, two important approaches have been developed (Pederson, Lonner, & Draguns, 1976).

Initially, the culture of the client was ignored. The counseling approach was determined by the theoretical orientation of the counselor. The client was treated with the techniques and from the personality conceptualization of that particular counselor's approach (Henderson, 1979). If the response to this treatment system was less than desirable, the client was usually labeled as resistant. This general approach to cultural differences received favorable counselor support since it placed no restrictions on the counselor's clientele.

By the mid-1960s, the culture-doesn't-matter viewpoint was under attack. The civil rights movement was in full swing and culturally different groups were demanding status and human rights. Specific culture studies soon became an important part of the curriculum of the full range of educational institutions (Atkinson, Morten, & Sue, 1979). Counselor education programs added courses purporting to teach consulting techniques designed for specific cultures. In some institutions, counseling specialization was equated to the cultural background of the counselor (e.g., the counselor of Hispanic heritage became the counselor of Hispanics).

Both of these traditional approaches to counseling the culturally different left something to be desired. In the culture-doesn't-matter approach, the shortcomings were readily apparent. This was particularly true for the client who was distinctly culturally different. For this person, the impact of culture was simply being ignored. Some counselors resisted efforts to scrap this viewpoint since many possessed no acceptable alternatives.

The approach of "you must be distinctly culturally different in order to help the culturally different" proved highly restrictive. Specifically, to say that White counselors could not help Black clients placed intolerable limits on counselors of all cultures. The response to these restrictions involved extensive efforts to inform counselors about the culturally different. Elaborate models were developed in efforts to assist counselors of one culture to be helpful to clients of different cultures. This response pattern proved inadequate in several areas.

1. The White culture was not identified and included in the curriculum. This oversight was fortuitous since the magnitude of this task was obvious.

2. Persons of mixed cultural heritage (perhaps a majority of Americans) were largely ignored.

3. Assumptions were made about distinctly culturally different groups and training programs were based on these assumptions. The individual differences within groups suffered considerably.

4. A heavy burden was placed on counselors who were themselves distinctly culturally different. The assumption was made that such a person possessed some magic and could work effectively with anyone.

A UNIQUE APPROACH

The counselor education faculty and students of the University of Nevada-Reno have attempted to approach the counseling of the culturally different from a more global viewpoint. As stated earlier, the assumption of this approach was that all persons are culturally different.

It was also assumed that culture was likely to play a major role in a person's affect, cognition, and behavior patterns (Walz & Benjamin, 1978). Also, the behavior that might be described as culture specific was considered to be learned. Further, most of this learning was acquired in social interaction within the individual culture. As a result, the specific counselor education emphasis as directed at the culturally different was based on social learning theory.

ACCULTURATION

The first step in counselor preparation was an examination of each student's acculturation process and a clarification of values acquired in that process. Students were asked to examine their ideas, feelings, and behavior patterns specific to culture. The examination was accomplished in three formats: personal introspection and writing, class group sharing, and individual interview. Harmin's (1974) "value sheets" were modified for use with adults and to the purpose of examining personal acculturation.

Most students struggle with a definition of culture, usually ending with broad statements such as "the say I do things." Many students are surprised to realize that they had not thought of themselves as culturally unique. Many find the process difficult because their culture is such a mixture of elements of various cultures.

In the process of studying their own and other cultures, students have identified examples of deculturation, specifically families in which historical cultural was not allowed to be expressed. In addition, institutions have been actively involved in the deculturation process (e.g., prisons and mental health treatment facilities where the deculturation process supposedly contributes to compliance).

An important function of the identification of personal culture is the demythologizing of people who are different. As students have studied their own cultures and those of others, they have come to see people as learning organisms. Thus, the distinctive aspects of other people became less mystical and more understandable. Culture became an important consideration in learning about others, and this learning process became an important part of the counselor education system.

COUNSELING APPROACH

The following is a brief overview of the counseling approach suggested for addressing issues involved in counseling culturally different individuals.

Relationship Development

The basic premise that all people are culturally different provides clues as to how relationships can be developed. The counselor cannot assume that one set of rapport-building behaviors will work with all people. Rather, counselors must be aware of their personal style and be sensitive to the responses of their clients. It seem apparent that the process of becoming aware and sensitive to self and others requires considerable effort. Activities from Simon's (1974) *Meeting Yourself Halfway* were found helpful in this process.

Data Gathering

Clients are the best source of data about their culture. Therefore, ways must be found to learn with clients about their personal culture and its impact on behavior. Counselors should be aware that clients frequently have not considered various aspects of their culture or its influence on their lives.

Counselors need to study a variety of approaches to learning about clients and cultures. To restrict the counseling process to an office and the interview system may place severe limitations on both counselor and client. Some clients may be reluctant to share specifics of their lifestyle and learning patterns, but this does not prohibit the counselor from observations and other learning tools.

Individual Counseling Strategies

The basic premise presented in this article is useful to counselors of any theoretical orientation. The individual counseling system or strategies can be enhanced by the recognition of the individual's culture. Knowledge of that culture and the behavioral manifestations should be helpful in any treatment mode.

Alternative Strategies for Help

Counselors should be aware that individual cultures may prohibit traditional counseling intervention with some people. In this event, counselors may themselves be more helpful by adopting consulting approaches or institutional change approaches.

A high school counselor found himself stymied in helping a group of students who were culturally similar and recently had been influenced by a few members of their group to demonstrate distrust of the school staff. The counselor found he was more helpful in becoming a consultant to parents and some previous graduates affiliated with this group. The counselor became a trainer, information provider, and situational consultant for the direct help providers.

In an industrial setting, a personnel counselor became aware of difficulties experienced by a particular group of employees. Limited use of English was severely restricting this group in productivity and in their efforts to advance. The counselor arranged with the local school district to provide adult classes in English instruction in the plant at a time convenient to these workers. The results were beneficial to the company and to the employees.

SUMMARY

This article suggests that counseling the culturally different be addressed from a premise that all people are culturally different. From that theoretical base, the counselor's primary focus is to learn about the individual culture of the client and the impact of culture on behavior.

Counselors who proceed from this premise must be well aware of their own culture and of their bias toward others. In addition, counselors must be sensitive to individual techniques for learning about client culture. To accomplish these goals of personal attitude adjustment, a variety of value clarification activities are used with counselors in pre-training and mid-career training.

The premise is that individual culture enhances all theories of counseling intervention, including consulting and institutional change approaches.

REFERENCES

Atkinson, D. R., Morten, G., & Sue, D. W. (1979). *Counseling American minorities*. Dubuque, Iowa: Brown.

Harmin, M. (1974). *Making sense of our lives—value sheets*. Niles, Ill.: Argus Communications.

Henderson, G. (Ed.). (1979). *Understanding and counseling ethnic minorities*. Springfield, Ill.: Charles C Thomas.

Pedersen, P, Lonner, W. J., & Draguns, J. G. (1976). *Counseling across cultures*. Honolulu: University of Hawaii Press.

Simon, S.B., Howe, L. W., & Kirschenbaum, H. (1972). *Values clarification*. New York: Hart.

Simon, S. E. (1974). *Meeting yourself halfway*. Niles, Ill.: Argus Communications.

Walz, G. R., & Benjamin, L. (1978). *Transcultural counseling: Needs, programs and techniques*. New York, Human Sciences Press.

Ethical Issues in Gerocounseling

**MARION L. CAVALLARO
MARYLOU RAMSEY**

COUNSELING FOR OLDER PERSONS has received increased attention in recent years because of the dramatic increase in the number of persons who are 65 years of age and older and their expanding need for information, as well as their growing requirements for assistance in adapting to personal, social, and technological change (Ricker, 1981). At the same time, much has been written concerning how counselors should interpret and apply the ethical guidelines of their profession to a variety of difficult practice situations (Corey, Corey, & Callahan, 1984). Unfortunately, to date there has been little discussion of combining the two areas, that is, aiding counselors in the development of an ethical attitude and position specific to gerontological counseling.

Current gerocounseling literature deals with the didactic information needed in understanding the problems and transitions of older persons, the strategies that help older persons deal with their concerns and live meaningful lives, and the roles and functions gerocounselors need to perform that are at variance with those traditionally characteristic of counselors (Ganikos, 1979). There has been little emphasis, however, on the unique ethical issues that correspond to such specialized practice.

A review of the literature pertinent to ethical issues and the elderly indicates that such issues have been addressed in the areas of nursing (Gunter, 1983), hospice care (Klagsburn, 1982), and long-term care (Moody, 1982). A common theme among these articles that is applicable to field of counseling is the importance of honoring informed consent with the elderly (Gunter, 1983; Moody, 1982). As interpreted by these authors, clients have the right to be active in any decision-making process that may affect them. Another issue raised is the importance of staff who work with the elderly to be sensitive to their own values and how these values might be in conflict with their work roles (Klagsburn, 1982).

Within the field of counseling, a recent article on ethical dilemmas in counseling elderly adults examines the theoretical ethical principles of fidelity, autonomy, and beneficence (Fitting, 1986). Fitting discusses the problems encountered in maintaining trust in a client-counselor relationship (fidelity), protecting the right of an individual to informed consent for treatment (autonomy), and helping people both by preventing harm and by actively intervening for positive benefit (beneficence). In determining which of these principles should be given the most importance, Fitting states that the final decision should be based on knowledge about elderly persons and their medical and health status, information about the psychological functioning and decision-making capability of elderly adults, and the AACD *Ethical Standards* (1981).

As members of the counseling profession, gerocounselors are guided by the *Ethical Standards* of the American Association for Counseling and Development (AACD, 1981); however, because these standards are generic for all counseling situations and client populations, there must be additional study and discussion on how to apply these standards to the unique ethical decisions faced in gerocounseling. Toward this end, this article will enumerate some of the ethical issues frequently encountered in gerocounselor practice, specifically, the issues of confidentiality, informed consent, dual relationships in counseling, and goals and values conflict. Each of these issues will be examined along with the AACD *Ethical Standards* that are pertinent, and suggested options for handling the conflicts will be made.

CONFIDENTIALITY

A highly debated ethical issue in gerocounseling is that of confidentiality. Ethical dilemmas often arise in determining how to handle information gleaned in certain counseling relationships with the elderly, especially those occurring in institutional settings. The AACD *Standards* (1981) hold that revelation to others of such information must occur only upon the expressed consent of the client or when there is clear and imminent danger to the client or others. Clear and imminent danger to the client or others is usually interpreted as situations in which the client may be suicidal or is threatening harm to another individual (Corey et al., 1984). This ethical code may place the gerocounselor in conflict in two different types of situations: (a) when the gerocounselor is summoned to service by a third party, for example, the family or an institutional authority, and not by the older client him or herself, and (b) when clients confide in counselors information regarding physical or mental abuse, unreported serious medical symptoms, or noncompliance with medical therapy that might adversely affect their well-being. Each of these issues will be examined separately.

Ethical issues are raised when the gerocounselor is asked to provide counseling to an older person by a third party, be it the family or an institutional authority (e.g, nursing home, hospital, or social service agency). In these situations, the third party may expect or desire information about the client that may be in conflict with the client's right to confidentiality. The counselor must then wrestle with questions such as "What, if anything, should be shared with the third party to promote the welfare of the client? What if there is no prospect for client resumption of responsibility? How long will counseling persist? What purposes will it serve, and how must the counselor's primary obligation be redefined?"

Ethical Issues in Gerocounseling

These issues can be addressed in a variety of ways. When a gerocounselor is hired by an institution, he or she should determine who the client is (some institutions take the position that if they pay the counselor's salary, then they are the client). If there are constraints placed on the gerocounselor's ability to maintain confidentiality because of the institution's perspective, then the client needs to be informed of these limits at the onset of counseling. Similarly, third parties, such as family members, should be apprised of the counselor's duty to maintain confidentiality when they make a request for counseling. In situations in which the client refuses counseling because of limitations placed on confidentiality, then alternative counseling resources should be recommended.

The second issue regarding confidentiality deals with conflicts raised when a client, particularly in an institutional setting, confides to a counselor information regarding physical or mental abuse, serious unreported medical symptoms, or noncompliance with medical therapy, and demands that this information not be shared with anyone. In case of physical or mental abuse, many states require that individuals who suspect that an elderly institutionalized person is being or has been mentally or physically abused report such information to a designated state office. Thus, the counselor could be in violation of state law and criminally liable if he or she does not breach confidentiality and report the information. In these instances, perhaps AACD *Ethical Standards* (1981) regarding breaking confidentiality only when there is clear and imminent danger to the client or others could be interpreted in accord with legal definitions to also include physical and mental abuse of an elderly person. Furthermore, counselors should ensure that their agency or institution has established reporting procedures for dealing with issues of abuse, and work with staff, family, and clients in understanding, recognizing, and knowing how to report these cases.

When dealing with issues such as serious unreported medical symptoms or noncompliance with medical therapy that could be life-threatening, counselors should be aware of their institution's policy regarding the reporting of such situations. In instances in which there are no relevant policies, counselors can work toward establishing them and then inform their clients if limits are placed on confidentiality in such cases.

INFORMED CONSENT

A controversial issue in gerocounseling is that of informed consent. According to AACD *Standards*, a counselor must inform the client of the purposes, goals, techniques, rules of procedure, and limitations of counseling at or before counseling commences, and when freedom of choice is curtailed, the client must be advised of such restrictions (AACD, 1981). In instances in which gerocounselors use related, less stigmatized titles, it can be argued that the consent to counseling that older clients give is only marginally valid, because such assistance is misrepresented or misunderstood.

Specifically, many older clients would not engage in counseling if it were presented as "therapy" because they may hold the historically and culturally conditioned belief that they should be mature enough to handle their own problems (Ganikos, 1979). Similarly, even in instances in which the elderly consent to counseling without its being retitled, the agreement can be riddled with misconceptions. For example, some elderly fear such a decision marks them as less capable or independent (Ganikos, 1979). Others believe counselors give advice, solve problems, and completely act on their behalf. Regardless of what the counselor states as the goals, procedures, and limitations of counseling, older people have more experience with—and expect—the direct medical helping model.

To ensure that elderly clients are giving knowledgeable consent to counseling services, gerocounselors could have their aged clients repeat back to them what they understand the counselor's role and function to be. In addition, this understanding could be conformed with a written and signed statement attesting to the nature of the relationship. Gerocounselors might want to assure their elderly clients that consent to counseling does not imply that they are any less capable and that their decision-making rights will be protected.

In institutional settings, the elderly may expect or prefer a medical helping model and, although capable of independent decision-making, may defer to medical staff or family members to make decisions for them, including whether to request or accept counseling services. In these settings, gerocounselors might consider providing inservice training to the staff, and educating family members on ways to preserve aged clients' decision-making rights. In addition, a team approach to care, which includes members of the medical, nursing, and counseling staff, as well as the client and family, would ensure that the client would be active in the decision-making processes that affect him or her and that all concerned parties would be working collaboratively for the benefit of the client.

In working with confused older clients, the issue of informed consent becomes particularly important. Previous authors (Fitting, 1986; Moody, 1982) have pointed out that legal means are not to be used to override a client's autonomy unless there is strong evidence of mental impairment. Protective services such as guardianship are not justified unless there is evidence of mental impairment; instances of chronic illness do not justify overriding the autonomy of the individual in decision making that affects his or her life. Therefore, the gerocounselor must make a careful assessment of the cognitive capacity of the individual to give his or her informed consent to counseling (Fitting, 1986). If the client is mentally impaired, permission for counseling should be secured from a responsible third party.

Conversely, in situations in which the guardian or family member requests counseling for a confused elder, the gerocounselor should be certain that such services are needed, and might consider seeing the confused elder once or twice informally to assess whether counseling is warranted. Even though the confused client is not the one responsible for giving informed consent to counseling, he or she still needs to be receptive to counseling. Thrusting counseling services on a confused older person who is resistant to the idea will not be conductive to establishing rapport and working towards change. Thus, the gerocounselor still needs to convince a confused client that counseling will be beneficial, and obtain acceptance of the idea from the client.

DUAL RELATIONSHIPS

AACD *Ethical Standards* indicate that when members have other relationships with clients, particularly of an administrative, supervisory, or evaluative nature, they must not serve as counselors for such individuals (AACD 1981). Only in situations in which other counseling services are not available should the members enter into a counseling relationship (AACD, 1981). In services to older people, staffing and funds are frequently limited and trained helping professionals may not be readily available. Often times, the person in the supervisor or administrator role is the only counselor available, and maintenance of such dual roles severely tests that individual's professional objectivity and ability to perform successfully.

Dual relationships in gerocounseling settings could be handled in a variety of ways. First, gerocounselors should clarify for themselves and to their clients their various roles and the extent and limits of their abilities to perform counseling services. Secondly, if possible, gerocounselors could establish separate physical locations or times for performance of each role. In this way, clients would know when or where to see the gerocounselor based on the nature of their concerns. Because clients can not always easily distinguish between counseling and administrative issues, gerocounselors need to be ready to "step out of role" when counseling, and remind clients of counseling limits prior to their revealing information that could create conflicts. Furthermore, outside referral resources for extensive counseling services should be utilized as much as possible. Finally, a client advocate could be engaged to listen to client's concerns, including potentially threatening material, and report back information to the gerocounselor or supervisor that requires administrative action while preserving the anonymity of the client.

GOALS AND VALUES CONFLICTS

A frequently mentioned ethical issue in gerocounseling involves conflicts between counselor's goals and values (Klagsburn, 1982). Counselors may be uncomfortable in dealing with issues older clients might raise involving dying, death, dependency, and religious concerns. For example, conflicting values between a counselor and client may arise concerning (a) a dying client's decision not to discuss death or the possibility of life sustaining options, or (b) a client with a terminal illness choosing to end his or her life. Counselors have been taught to help clients explore presenting concerns, and they may have difficulty responding to individuals who desire not to discuss personal circumstances. Concomitant with such goal conflicts, counselors may also find that their values regarding caring for the dying and self-sufficiency are at odds with those of their clients. The client may perceive death with dignity as dying at home without people attending to him or her, or may become very spiritual, placing his or her fate in God's hands. If the counselor views dying at home as neglecting the client, or has difficulty accepting religious beliefs, discussions surrounding such issues will be problematic.

Gerocounselors need to consider a number of alternatives when dealing with goals and values conflicts. First, if a gerocounselor is particularly uncomfortable with the values issues being presented to the extent that it is interfering with counselor objectivity, then referral to another counselor should be made. Secondly, formal didactic and experimental training and consultation and supervision should be pursued in sensitive areas such as death and dying. Furthermore, gerocounselors should become familiar with different cultural perspectives regarding aging, death, and dying so that they can understand and support their clients in a culturally sensitive manner.

In addition to being aware of cultural factors, gerocounselors should recognize individual differences and preferences regarding the way a person choose to both live and die and be able to support clients in their choices. When clients choose to die at home, and this choice is contrary to that of the counselor, the counselor should still be able to support the client by mobilizing resources from the family and the community to assist the client. Finally, gerocounselors must recognize that serving as their clients' advocate regarding needs and values often becomes necessary. Thus, gerocounselors should become familiar with advocacy strategies and legal movements (e.g., living wills) that will support them in protecting their clients' rights and choices.

CONCLUSION

The ethical issues mentioned are certainly not all-encompassing in number. Those issues addressed in this issue primarily focused on ethical dilemmas that arise from the counselor-client relationship. As the gerocounseling field grows, new issues pertaining to both the counselor-client relationship and organizational practices will arise. Counselors will need to be increasingly sensitive to these issues, aware of the AACD *Ethical Standards* (1981) that apply, and actively engaged in responding to such ethical dilemmas in a consistent, responsible fashion.

REFERENCES

American Association for Counseling and Development. (1981). *Ethical Standards.* Alexandria VA: Author. (originally published by the American Personnel and Guidance Association)

Corey, G., Corey, M. S., & Callahan, P. (1984). *Issues and ethics in the helping professions* (3rd ed.). Monterey, CA: Brooks/Cole.

Fitting, M. D. (1986). Ethical dilemmas in counseling elderly adults. *Journal of Counseling and Development, 64,* 325–327.

Ganikos, M. L. (Ed.). (1979). *Counseling the aged: A training syllabus for educators.* Washington, DC: American Personnel and Guidance Association.

Gunter, L. M. (1983). Ethical considerations for nursing care of older patients in the acute care setting. *Nursing Clinics of North America, 18*(2), 411–421.

Klagsburn, S. C. (1982). Ethics in hospice care. *American Psychologist, 34*(11), 1263–1265.

Moody, H. (1982). Gerontological social work practice in long-term care: Ethical dilemmas in long-term care. *Journal of Gerontological Social Work, 5,*(1–2), 97–111.

Ricker, H. C. (1981). Gerontological counseling. In J. E. Myers, P. Finnerty-Fried, & C. H. Graves (Eds.), *Counseling older persons. Vol. 1: Guidelines for a team approach to training* (pp. 3–10). Falls Church, VA: American Personnel and Guidance Association.

Object Relations and the Development of Values

GEORGE M. GAZDA
CHARALEE SEDGWICK

VALUES ACQUISITION IS a process that is reflected in the transferential aspect of the therapeutic relationship. Specifically, the mechanisms by which a client generally adopts values is reflected in his or her adoption of the therapist's values. Furthermore, when a client adopts the values of his or her therapist, that client has previously identified, then idealized, and finally acknowledged the reality of the therapist. To explain how this happens, we present the etiology of identification, because it is the basis of value formation. Identification gives rise to idealizing, developmentally speaking; thus, idealizing in turn will be addressed because it is a pivotal part of the dynamic that has the client adopting the therapist's values.

Basic also to this article is the premise that identification, and the consequent assumption of a value, results from an emotional tie between two people. It is necessary at this point to make a distinction between beliefs and values. Beliefs are classically considered to be cognitive, whereas values are associated with the affective dimension of personality; values, in other words, reflect feelings and are played out in behavior.

It is important to be mindful of this difference between beliefs and values when examining the observations others have made about the influence of therapists' values on clients (e.g., Beutler, 1971a, 1971b, 1979a, 1979b; Frank, 1973; Goldstein, Heller, & Sechrist, 1966). Values are considered with regard to the following classical definition: Values emerge from the affective and behavioral realm, and they are more powerfully communicated unconsciously than cognitively. Overall, it is the emotional tone of the relationship, the capacity of the client to experience the therapeutic relationship as a safe *holding environment* (Winnicott, 1965) that, ultimately, provides the right atmosphere for identifying with whatever values the therapist may exemplify.

IDENTIFICATION

The tendency of a person to idealize another is based on an earlier time in which that person was involved in the developmental task of developing a conscience, or to express it psychoanalytically, a superego. Patterson (1958) said that, in the process whereby the client absorbs the values of the therapist, there is the new formation of a superego patterned after that of the therapist. Thus, developmentally speaking, because a person's conscience develops between ages 5 and 8, the need to idealize comes as a later phase to earlier identifications, which begin to occur soon after birth. We also describe how at that earlier time, a certain patterning of the more basic ego is a result of identifying processes.

Every child, as he or she moves through the various developmental stages, is moved to identify with important others. When that happens, aspects of identification come into play as parts of a process that eventually determines the person's uniqueness—a sense of himself or herself as an individual. This self-knowledge comes by way of a relationship; the "I," in other words, begins and evolves in the context of a "we." A series of identifications characterizes this process of individuation.

The earliest kind of identification is a product of the baby's sorting out and defining different aspects of his or her world. This process of definition is related to the baby's efforts to determine what is good about his or her environment and what is bad or what food is tasty and should be swallowed and what should be spit out. At this point in the infant's development, it is not so much a matter that he or she perceives himself of herself differently from the parent. It is more a matter of the infant's perceiving differences in his or her environment and trying to classify those differences in terms of pleasure and pain. The child tries to absorb what he or she perceives as good (introjection) and reject what is bad (projection). These psychological mechanisms are a precursor of what Kernberg (1979) called *splitting*, when the infant, through normal development, is beginning to discriminate elements of his or her world.

Freud (1955) spoke of the interplay between a feeling of "oneness" and differentiation in a broader context. The child, from his or her viewpoint, experiences a feeling of oneness with both parents from the very beginning by sharing common experiences with them. At the same time, the child is learning to differentiate the parents from one another by having different relationships with each one. Later, the child chooses to identify with the parent of the same sex because of common experiences shared with that parent, returning to a "feeling of oneness." This experience of oneness is, according to Freud, one of the motivating forces behind a person's tendency to identify.

Intrapsychically, differentiation among parts of the infant's world serves to define that world but creates an ambivalence in the child as time passes. The child's ambivalence in the earlier period now, at 18 to 24 months, escalates into a pronounced distress, known as the *rapproachment crises* (Mahler, Pine, & German, 1975). Now the rebellious toddler experiences an inner pressure to develop autonomous ego functions. No longer is the toddler as accepting of the different behaviors of his or her mother, which are clumped under two rubrics, good and bad, and which, for him or her, have been interpreted as two people, the "good" and "bad" mothers. The toddler is now moved to combine into one person the two aspects of mother that he or she has experienced. By integrating the different parts of mother, that is, seeing her as one person made up of different behaviors, a child begins to experience his or her own self as whole. As a parallel process, the child experiences more and more of his or her own autonomy when recognizing the parent as more separate and multidimensional than before.

Children accomplish this autonomy via what Kohut (1971) called *transmuting internalization*, a process in which they incorporate the interactions between themselves and the parent. In the relationship, children achieve a sense of themselves in contrast to the parent—"you are you, and I am I." As they become aware of their differences, they simultaneously become aware of what passes between themselves and that parent—what the interactions are in the relationship. Children do not have the urge to swallow the parent whole, as the infant does; instead, at this time children introject the interactions between themselves and parents. For example, toddlers absorb the mother's calming function, which means they are now learning to calm themselves when she is not available to do it. By the same token, the baby can separate from her when it is necessary, when her soothing and comforting seem smothering, by internalizing the experience of the "bad" mother (named thus by virtue of the fact that the child perceived her as "bad" when she was not gratifying). Because toddlers can now bring up in themselves the two different aspects of mother, this means that now they are beginning to experience themselves as truly whole. When this inner work is done, the toddler's experience of separateness does not depend on outer events. This is how the achievement of mastery (echoed in toddling achievements) is played out intrapsychically and results in the formation of the ego.

This process of introjection just described is not the same as an identifying act. Introjection precedes identification; object relations create conditions conducive to identification.

> Introjection increases the similarity between the subject and the lost object by altering the ego of the subject after the pattern of the object. Thus, introjection creates all conditions of similarity necessary for identification . . . identification is the result of introjection. (Day, 1961, p. 15)

The fruits of the identification that occurred at separation/individuation appear in the imitations of the parent. Imitation is just an obvious manifestation of identification. According to Freud (195), imitation represents an urge to both be and take the place of an admired object. He describes the son's imitation of his father as his wish "to grow like him and be like him and take his place everywhere" (p. 678). "Taking his place everywhere" implies not only the idea of *oneness* mentioned before, but also the ideal of a *reciprocal relationship*, which, as we shall demonstrate later, distinguishes identifying from idealizing.

Three- to 5-year-old children fine tune the massive identifications of pre-oedipal years, identifying with particular aspects of those they love, dressing up like Mommy, for example, or learning to "police" themselves the way their parents do. These partial and selective identifications are important developmentally not only because of the establishment of sexual identity and further growth in the area of object relations, but because of an increasing ability of the child to synthesize and integrate mental impressions. The constant revamping of identifications that goes on at this time contributes to a mental need children experience to organize impressions of themselves under more abstract rubrics. This emergence of a transcendent and uniquely personal schema is the beginning of the child's awareness of his or her values.

IDENTIFICATION AND IDEALIZATION

Identification is different from idealization in that the former is a condition in which a person is recognized by another for being what he or she really is. When one person idealizes an other, however, the one doing the idealizing attributes to the other person qualities that she or he does not have. This is the psychological mechanism known as projection, and it is at the heart of the transference phenomenon. A person's identifying tendencies, then, become transferential in nature when he or she begins to idealize others.

According to Freud (1955), a person's tendency to identify arises from an attraction to something similar in another person, which is for the most part based on common experience. Identification, therefore, involves a mutuality; the individual perceives himself or herself and the other to be basically alike. Identification is, among other things, an act of definition, of clarification, as has been described earlier in its etiology.

When one person idealizes another, however, he or she looks up to another person—it is not an equal relationship. Idealizing someone is to put that person above oneself; that is, to be "one down" in relation to the person idealized. This relationship is not meant to be equal, however. Identification turns into idealization as the result of a developmental deficit. It is a condition that reflects past influence, echoing old interactions (or a lack of them) with a parent. Idealizing, then, is a manner of relating that implies transference because of the parent-child interaction it suggests.

Idealizing figures prominently as a developmental phenomenon at the time in which the conscience, or superego, is being formed. At that time, children are not so much defining themselves as they are in the process of construing values. Simultaneously, children look up to significant others in their lives for help in this effort. The child sees his or her parents with the eyes of the world, watches them move through their milieu with the approval or disapproval of others. He or she perceives whether or not the parent is, in fact, loved by others, and if so, this reinforces the child's developing sense of being socially fit because he or she, too, loves that parent.

Along with the development of this social component, the child's values are born out of the loving interaction with that parent. For example, a child may come to value honesty. This may be essentially because he or she felt cared for and attended to when the parent was honest. A little boy may perceive his father as being brave, and may aspire to be brave himself someday. This aspiration, more than likely, was born out of an emotional memory when the boy was protected by his father from evils imagined or real, times when the boy felt the father's soothing.

The one-up configuration of the idealizing relationship is important in terms of the establishment of values. One reason for this involves the transcendent quality of values. Values, by definition, are mental artifacts born of emotional interactions with others that represent what people aspire to be. Some individuals look for the clarification of their own values in other people whom they perceive to be superior, more "advanced" than themselves. Unlike identification, which has people recognizing similarities, idealizing involves one's perception of someone else as a model, as a carrier of qualities the idealizer wishes to have.

VALUES AND THE IDEALIZING TRANSFERENCE

When a client idealizes a therapist, he or she presupposes that the therapist has certain values. This situation is a combined one of a transference and a parallel relationship based on real, or nonprojected, elements. The focus here will be on an aspect of reality that Kohut (1971) called *optimal frustration*. He used this term to refer to an important dynamic that occurs between therapist and client in the framework of an idealizing transference. There are times when encountering the reality of the therapist is a disagreeable experience for any client who is caught up in an idealization of that therapist. The therapist may be 5 minutes late or inappropriately say or not say something, and for the client who idealizes, the trivial fault is magnified into a catastrophe. Like 5-year-old children, clients are for the moment caught off balance with the realization that the "parent" is not perfect. To regain equilibrium, clients use memory in an important way. They recall the basic substance of the relationship, the empathetic tone of past interactions. In this way, they reassure themselves that all is well, basically, between themselves and their therapist.

In this reaction to disappointment described above, memory serves the client in a particular way. When the client is optimally frustrated, he or she remembers former interactions with the therapist rather than the personality of that therapist. Memory eases the frustration in a psychological mechanism that Kohut (1971) called *transmuting internalization*. Here, the functions the therapist has served for the client are internalized. In the development of the child, transmuting internalization occurs when the child begs to be picked up and soothed, and for some reason the mother cannot respond.

The child must then draw on the memory of the mother and must remember her soothing presence in times past to soothe himself or herself. This internalization process, as described by Kohut, is not simply the child's swallowing aspects of the parent whole; it is based on the tension of their relationship:

> While the child idealizes the parent, the idealized constellation is open to correction and modification through actual experience (the child's recognition of the actual qualities of the parents), and the empathic parents' gradual revelation of their shortcomings enables the child . . . to withdraw a part of the idealizing libido from the parental images and to employ them in the building up of drive-controlling structures. (Kohut, 1971, p. 41)

This idea of transmuting internalization is basic to Kohut's conception of the growth of the self. It is based on one's perception of the real elements of the person being idealized. The mother has frustrated the child, not deliberately, but because of the realities of her life; this frustration, Kohut's optimal frustration, begins the motion of transmuting internalization. The child takes in her soothing function and can use it then to comfort himself or herself. Like the toddler, the client will struggle with the frustration of being disappointed and will pass thorough it, drawing on previous memories of the therapist in earlier therapeutic exchanges that were important.

When the toddler internalizes the function of the mother, the quality absorbed is not hers alone but something experienced between the two of them. The toddler is a necessary participant; the mother's soothing makes no sense unless the toddler is there to be soothed. So it is with the client. The "stuff" that clients internalize, after tying to "right" themselves in the face of frustration, is not only the memory of the bond between themselves and their therapists but also the appendages to the bond (i.e., the values they projected into the therapist). Those values become emblematic of the basic experience of bonding; they become signposts, in a sense, that serve to remind the client of the underlying interaction. Recall the idealizing little boy who wants to be brave like his father. He thinks of the times when it felt good to be protected and then he remembers how his father was at those times. By way of an association, then, the quality of bravery is internalized as an ideal by the youngster, who remembers first how it felt good to be protected and then remembers why.

The second point essential to this idea of internalization is the part referred to in the above quote as "the empathic parents' gradual revelation of their shortcomings." That part of the process creates in the child the optimal frustration referred to above. This frustration contributes to the structure of the self via the energy that is created when the child's ideal parent and the real parent clash. The parent, in other words, is not doing anything in particular to frustrate the child; the parent is just behaving normally. And in the course of doing so, the parent somehow disappoints the child. The "shortcoming" of the parent, then, motivates the child to withdraw a bit of the idealization from the parent and take it back into himself or herself. When this child takes the bit of idealization back, he or she forms a value, such as bravery, to hang it on.

In the therapeutic situation, some clients, as a result of not having successfully completed for themselves a primary set of values by age 10, tend to idealize the therapist because of a need to finish up the unfinished inner project. The condition of idealizing is a dead giveaway that the idealizer is caught in a past condition. The quality being perceived and admired is the projector's own. At some pivotal point in the therapeutic relationship, the therapist will disappoint the client, not purposefully, but in the course of normal behavior. When the reality of the person being projected upon clashes with the quality itself, the client suffers a dissonance that propels him or her to do something with the quality that, for the time being, doesn't fit the therapist. It is at this time that the client internalizes that quality and names it as a value. The client then claims for himself or herself those values that were projected and unconscious if the relationship with the therapist is good enough; that is, if the therapeutic relationship has enough empathy, shared understanding, and consistency, these fundamental processes will most likely occur. This is a convincing explanation for there being, in the main, an emotional component to a value; the assumption of values, in the past as in the present, rests on an emotional exchange between two people.

SUMMARY

The acquisition of values is directly related to the successes and failures of early relationships. Beginning with the infant's desire to "swallow" the beloved parent, the individual develops a sense of what he or she values by moving through a series of identifications. In this article we have described the steps a person goes through in making identifications, explaining the steps that move the person toward the construction of a value system. In particular, special attention has been paid to the condition of idealizing, the final level in development identification. By referring to the work of Heinz Kohut, we have explained how the child's idealizing has within it necessary components for his or her growth in individuation.

In the context of the client-therapist relationship, the idealizing transference becomes the vehicle for the re-experiencing of old, unfinished admiration. Inasmuch as an adult never completed the business of constructing a framework of early values for himself or herself, so will that adult be inclined to project those unfinished parts of an idealizing relationship onto the therapist. Reasons then surface that explain why the original act of idealizing was unsuccessful. Much of the original interaction is experienced and interpreted, hinging on the two major aspects of the idealizing transference that Kohut called optimal frustration and transmuting internalization. This article focuses on the mechanics of these two psychological processes because, from a psychodynamic position, it is through these that a person's values are identified and established.

REFERENCES

Beutler, L. E. (1971a). Attitude similarity in marital therapy. *Journal of Consulting and Clinical Practice, 37*, 298–301.

Beutler, L. E. (1971b). Predicting outcomes of psychotherapy: A comparison of predictions from two theories. *Journal of Consulting and Clinical Psychology, 37*, 411–416.

Beutler, L. E. (1979a). Values, beliefs, religion, and the persuasive influence of psychotherapy. *Psychotherapy: Theory, Research, and Practice, 16*, 432–440.

Beutler, L. E. (1979b). Individual, group, and family therapy modes: Patient-therapist value compatibility and treatment effectiveness. *Journal of Consulting and Clinical Psychology, 2*, 43–59.

Day, G. D. (1961). *An exploration of the theory of identification, with an experimental investigation of its operation in oral communication.* Unpublished master's thesis, University of Illinois, Urbana.

Frank, J. D. (1973). *Persuasion and healing: A comparative study of psychotherapy* (rev. ed.). Baltimore: Johns Hopkins University Press.

Freud, S. (1955). Group psychology and analysis of the ego. In J. Stratchey (Ed.), *The standard edition of the complete psychological works of Sigmund Freud* (Vol. 18, pp. 100–111). London: Hogarth Press. (Original work published 1921)

Goldstein, A. P., Heller, K., & Sechrist, L. B. (1966). *Psychotherapy and the psychology of behavior change.* New York: Wiley.

Kernberg, O. (1979). *Borderline conditions and pathological narcissism.* New York: Jason Aronson.

Kohut, H. (1971). *The analysis of the self.* New York, International Universities Press.

Mahler, M. S., Pine, F., & Bergman, A. (1975). *The psychological birth of the human infant.* New York: Basic Books.

Patterson, C. H. (1958). The place of values in counseling and psychotherapy. *Journal of Counseling Psychology, 5*, 216–223.

Winnicott, D. W. (1964). *The maturational processes and the facilitating environment.* New York: International Universities Press.

The Impact of Contemporary Idealogy and AIDS on the Counseling of Gay Clients

JAMES RUDOLPH

MINISTERING TO the psychotherapy needs of homosexuals has historically been an exercise in dissatisfaction and discomfort for many clients and counselors. Gay psychotherapy is as complex as the larger issue of gay self-determination is controversial; gay psychotherapy cannot exist in a vacuum apart from the society in which it is practiced. The counselor is as much a member of the society in which he or she is cultivated as is any other person and, thus, is equally vulnerable to the social and political influences of that society. I propose that three influences, all emerging in the past decade, have had both obvious and subtle negative effects on counselors' attitudes toward homosexuality and a destructive effect on gay psychotherapy: (a) the widespread acceptance of a conservative political ideology, (b) the return to prominence of fundamentalist religiosity, and (c) the appearance of Acquired Immune Deficiency Syndrome (AIDS).

THE SCOPE OF GAY PSYCHOTHERAPY

If one accepts the seminal 10% epidemiological statistic generated by Kinsey (Kinsey, Pomeroy, & Martin, 1948; Kinsey, Pomeroy, Martin & Gebhard, 1953) and replicated by others (Churchill, 1967; National Organization for Women, cited in Kingdon, 1979), 22 million individuals in the current population of the United States can be considered either predominantly or exclusively homosexual in nature. Because of such diverse problems as an increased rate of being assault victims, employment and housing discrimination, poor self-esteem, feelings of regret about being gay, alcoholism and other drug dependence, and increased incidences of depression, tension, loneliness, worry, and suicidal ideation and gesturing (Bell & Weinberg, 1978; Escoffier, 1975; Hart et al., 1978; Levine, 1980; Levitt & Klassen, 1974; Moses & Hawkins, 1982; Saghir, Robins, Walbran, & Gentry, 1970a), gay persons proportionately seek psychotherapy more frequently than do heterosexual persons (Bell & Weinberg, 1978; Saghir et al., 1970a; 1970b).

But there is often little satisfaction for the gay client in psychotherapy (Bell & Weinberg, 1978; Fisher, 1972; Gold, 1973; Kameny, 1972; Killinger, 1971; Moses & Hawkins, 1982; Tripp, 1975; West, 1977; Woodman & Lenna,

1982). I believe a major source of this psychotherapy failure lies in prejudicial counselor attitudes, which are formed from antigay sociocultural sentiments that have become more pervasive and are communicated either consciously or unwittingly to gay clients.

THE SWING TO A CONSERVATIVE SOCIOPOLITICAL IDEOLOGY

In the past decade, the United States has experienced a consistent shift to a more conservative sociopolitical ideology, with the most evident confirmations of such a transition being Ronald Reagan's 1980 and 1984 landslide presidential victories. Since the mid-1970s, there has been a stable increase in the absolute and relative numbers of adult Americans identifying themselves as politically conservative (Gallup, 1975b; 1979; 1982d; 1984b; National Opinion Research Center, 1985), with the Harris Survey (1986) reporting for the first time since 1968, and with a plurality of 40%, that more adult Americans identify themselves as conservative than either moderate (38%) or liberal (18%). As Kopkind (1984) noted perceptively, "The day has passed when just the 'conservative' label was enough to discredit its bearer. Nowadays, it is worn proudly whereas 'liberal' has become the pejorative of choice" (p. 450).

The "new right" represents a return to "traditional American" values. Stacks (1981) reported the results of a national survey on values conducted by *Time* that strongly supported the shift to sociopolitical conservatism: 70% of those surveyed agreed government has become too involved in individuals' personal lives, 60% said they believe that the media are too permissive and insufficiently moral; and 71% stated that the Supreme Court and Congress have overextended their mandates in excluding religious and moral value from individuals' personal lives. Of those adults polled by Gallup in 1977, 45% believed there should be stricter standards for sexually explicit material, and 66% believed most persons do not lead moral lives (Gallup, 1977a). Of those polled in 1982, 47% (Gallup, 1982b) believed it important to follow a strict moral code; 67% responded they would not welcome greater acceptance in society of sexual freedom (Gallup, 1982a); and in 1986, 37% supported traditional (conservative) rather than moderate (liberal) sexual, family life, and religious values (Gallup, 1986). As Fairlie (1982) noted, there is a public concern about the absence of firm social values, and "All that is represented by flag and family and God is felt to be in danger" (p. 17).

It is this reappearance of traditional values that bodes ominously for gay self-determination. Throughout American history, homosexuality has been neither accepted nor tolerated, but instead has been consistently suppressed and persecuted (Bayer, 1981; Beane 1981; Brudnoy, 1976). In contemporary times, the new right has exerted a formative influence in fashioning the 1984 National Republican Platform, which denied gay rights, as well as the 1986

Supreme Court decision upholding Georgia's antisodomy statute. Such developments seem to be as instructive as they are sobering for the cause of gay self-determination. As Church (1986) appropriately observed in response to the high court's ruling, "The times they are a changin' . . . in a way never forecast by Bob Dylan" (p. 24). Kopkind (1984) noted that "Reaganism" takes ideas, personnel, and energies from the "straight male hostility to . . . gay rights" (p. 449), and it would be misleading to underestimate the influence of the President's "stunning" victories or the "astounding unanimity" of the American public in support of many of his policies (Rosenblatt, 1984, p. 36). As White (1984) incisively concluded, Reagan will be remembered above all as an individual who shaped the values and moralities of this time, and indeed, as Church (1984) further noted, Reagan's conservative sociopolitical ideology "holds more sway than anyone could have guessed" (p. 39). It does not seem unreasonable to assume this is as true for counselors as it is for others.

THE REVIVAL OF FUNDAMENTALIST RELIGIOSITY

America has been referred to as a "nation with the soul of a church" ("A Time for," 1977, p. 56). This seems to be a fair statement when the following Gallup research data encompassing the previous decade is considered: percentage of respondents who attend weekly church services (1975a, 40%; 1976, 40%; 1977a, 42%, 1982c, 41%; 1984a, 40%); believe religion is increasing its influence in American life (1975a, 31%; 1976; 39%; 1977a, 44%; 1982c, 38%; 1984a, 44%; 1985, 48%); believe religion can answer today's problems (1975a, 62%; 1985, 61%); consider themselves to be very or fairly religious (1975a, 89%); believe themselves to be "born again" (1977a, 34%; 1982c, 35%); favor a constitutional amendment that supports allowing prayer in the public schools (1980, 76%); would welcome religious beliefs playing a greater role in people's lives (1982a, 76%); believe in the importance of following God's will (1982b, 61%); and who state that religion is extremely important in their personal lives (1982c, 56%; 1984a, 56%; 1985, 56%).

Ostling (1985) reported approximately 1,000 of the 9,642 radio stations in this country use a religious format (most of these are fundamentalist or evangelical), and 13 million persons regularly view religious television programs in the United States. It seems that, as an article in the *National Review* (1984) stated, "America is experiencing a tremendous religious revival . . . it is vital, growing, powerful" ("A Christian Country?", p. 18).

Fundamentalist doctrine and practice have historically been, and remain, a substantial source of antigay sentiment. Bullough (1979) considered Judeo-Christian doctrine to be the singular most important force in the formulation of western attitudes toward homosexuality, and Weinberg (1972) noted that it was not until ecclesiastic powers were engaged that oppression of homosexuals became "most atrocious" (p. 9; for further discussion see also Bayer,

1981; Bell & Weinberg, 1978; Moses & Hawkins, 1982: Nelson, 1982; West, 1977; Woodman & Lenna, 1982)

Gallup (1977b) reported that those who attend and are members of a church are far more likely to harbor antigay sentiment than are those who do not attend or are not members. Gallup noted such differences were among the most dramatic in this particular survey and concluded that, ironically, it is partly because Americans are a highly religious people that homosexuals encounter such difficulty in this country. Furthermore, the fundamentalist and evangelical religious denominations—those condemning homosexuality most stridently—are experiencing the greatest growth in membership ("Protestants: Away from," 1977).

The respective phenomena of the new political right and the resurgence of fundamental religiosity have united to form a synergistic entity labeled by Carey (1984) as the "Christian right" (p. 129) or the "religious right" (Andersen, 1984, p. 9). The influence of this union has been, and remains, extensive. Through such organizations as Jerry Falwell's Moral Majority and American Coalition for Traditional Values and the National Right to Life Committee, liberal, or otherwise unacceptable, political candidates have been targeted for defeat in past national, state, and local elections (with evident success in certain cases). Ostling (1985) noted that the Moral Majority has repeatedly used the issue of gay rights in its direct-mail fund-raising campaigns, and it has been perceptively observed, if ironically phrased, that "Religious conviction is 'out of the closet' in the national consciousness, with secular and religious consequences yet to be measured" ("A Time for," 1977, p. 54).

THE IMPACT OF AIDS

It would be difficult to overestimate the extent to which AIDS has affected the collective consciousness of the American people, particularly regarding its association with homosexuality. Gallup (1983a) reported that 77% of those surveyed had either heard of or read about AIDS; 45% believed no cure would be found in the next few years; and 43% believed AIDS would reach epidemic proportions. Thomas (1985) reported the results of a CBS-*New York Times* poll in which more respondents cited AIDS as the most serious medical problem currently facing the country than cited heart disease, the reported leading cause of death in the United States. The American public is well aware of the existence of AIDS and views it as a clear and present danger.

The association of AIDS with gay persons has become virtually reflexive, obviously because of the much publicized fact that most AIDS sufferers are homosexual men. AIDS is repeatedly referred to as the "gay plague" (Wallis, 1985), and there is considerable concern in the homosexual community that progress in gay self-determination may be irreparably harmed by the association (Clark, 1985; Leerhsen, 1985; Thomas, 1985). Morrow (1985) wrote eloquently, as follows, of this concern in an essay titled "The Start of a Plague Mentality":

> Because 73% of those who have AIDS are homosexuals, the general populace tends to look with suspicion on all homosexuals. . . . In most minds, a vague dread of the disease is accompanied by a sympathy for those afflicted. Sympathy, alas, is usually directly proportional to one's distance from the problem, and the sentiment will recede if the virus spreads and the sympathetic become the threatened. (p. 92)

A counselor can become as threatened as any other person.

In conclusion, pertinent survey research directly addressing the issue of homosexuality and popular opinion merits attention: the percentage of respondents who believe a homosexual cannot be a good Christian of Jew (33%, Gallup, 1977b); believe homosexuality is more pervasive than in the past (66%, Gallup. 177b); believe homosexual relations should not be legal (43%, Gallup, 177b; 39%, 1982e); do not accept homosexuality as an alternative lifestyle (51%, Gallup, 1982e); would not vote for a gay person for president (64%, Gallup, 1983b); and believe sex education courses should tell students that homosexuality is immoral (56%, Leo, 1986). According to the National Opinion Research Center (1985), the percentage of respondents who believe homosexual relations between two adults is always wrong is on the increase: 1974, 67%; 1976, 67%; 1977, 68%; 1980, 70%; 1982, 70%; 1984, 70%; and 1985, 73%. Thus, the collective survey data, with but few exceptions, indicates that a substantial and growing set of negative attitudes about homosexuality are being held by most individuals in this country.

THE COUNSELOR AND THE GAY CLIENT

Studies investigating attitudes of human service personnel, including psychotherapists, toward homosexuality have resulted in conflicting outcomes. Certain studies have reported either clearly antigay attitudes found in the samples or have implied the existence of such by reporting positive attitude change as a function of various treatments (e.g., Anderson, 1981; Barr & Catts, 1974; Casas, Brady, & Ponterotto, 1984; Clark, 1979; Davison & Wilson, 1973; Douglas, Kalman, & Kalman, 1985; Fischer, 1982; Hyman, 1980; McCann-Winter, 1983; Morris, 1973). It is easy to speculate why gay clients express dissatisfaction with the services rendered to them by antigay personnel; individuals who hold prejudicial attitudes may well be expected to provide less than helpful service. The origins of such negative attitudes involve the sociocultural phenomena discussed in this article, in addition to a myriad of others (cf. Bullough & Bullough, 1977; Bullough, 1979; Bell & Weinberg, 1978; Ivey, 1972; Killinger, 1971; MacDonald, 1976; McIntosh, 1968; Norton, 1982; Nuehring, Fein, & Tyler, 1974; West, 1977).

Contrasting with the studies documenting antigay attitudes of human service personnel is a second set of studies typified by the following reports.

Gartrell, Kraemer, and Brodie (1974) surveyed 390 psychiatrists regarding their attitudes toward female homosexuality: 98% favored legalization of homosexual relations between consenting adults; 66% opposed the psychiatric classification of female homosexual behavior; and 87% stated that a psychologically well-adjusted woman could be gay. Pauly and Goldstein (1970) reported that only 28% of the 937 physicians they surveyed believed their attitudes toward homosexuality adversely affected their medical treatment of gay patients; in a poll of more than 27,700 psychiatric and nonpsychiatric physicians, two-thirds of the respondents stated they were in favor of legalizing homosexual acts between consenting adults ("Poll on Socio-Medical," 1969). According to a survey by Fort, Steiner, and Conrad (1971), 64% of 163 psychotherapists stated they did not consider homosexuality to be a disease, and 98% believed it was possible for homosexuals to function effectively. Finally, Roman, Charles, and Karasu (1978) reported that 67% of 124 psychotherapists believed homosexual experience was acceptable for others (although only 4% stated such experience was acceptable for themselves).

Studies investigating gay clients' reactions to their psychotherapy experiences, however, suggest them to be frequently less than positive. Momentarily dismissing the negative effects of those psychotherapists who are clearly antigay (as Riddle & Sang, 1978, noted, "The one advantage of [such] therapists . . . is that they can be avoided," p. 92), the issue becomes one of accounting for the discrepancy between stated psychotherapist neutrality toward, or even support, of homosexuality on the one hand, and gay client dissatisfaction with psychotherapy, on the other. The literature indicates gay clients' dissatisfaction to be based on their perceptions of negative prejudicial attitudes toward, and a lack of understanding of, homosexuality by counselors. What is it that transpires in a session between ostensibly neutral, or even positive counselors and their gay clients, (apparently without the counselor's awareness), that nonetheless has such a damaging influence? Counselors are apparently acquiring and communicating prejudicial sentiments and lack of understanding to the gay clients they treat without being aware that they are doing so.

It seems instructive to briefly consider two studies investigating the phenomena of subliminal perception, incident learning, and the acquisition of prejudicial attitudes, because the mechanisms examined in such investigations may elucidate the discrepancy at hand. In a classic study by Greenspoon (1955), 75 undergraduate students were instructed to say all the words they could think of for 50 minutes. Whenever the participants would emit plural responses, the experimenter would verbalize "Mmm-hmm;" whenever the participants would emit nonplural responses, the experimenter would respond with "Huh-uh." The results revealed that "Mmmhmm" significantly increased, and "Huh-uh" significantly decreased, the frequency of participants' plural and nonplural responses, respectively. Most of the participants (87%) were unable to verbalize the relationship between the contingent stimulus and the response it followed.

Goethals and Reckman (1973) reported a study in which 18 high school students were placed in discussion groups in which a confederate of the experimenter was planted to argue the opposite view from that held by group participants on the social issue of busing. Many participants in both experimental groups changed their attitudes, although at debriefing, they indicated that the positions they adopted after the discussions were the same as those they had always held. The participants reported that the discussion groups had not changed their positions on the issue, and no one in the groups had influenced their positions.

Although other examples of subliminal perception and imperceptible learning could be listed (e.g., Bem & McConnell, 1970; Latane & Darley, 1970; Nisbett & Wilson, 1977), the above sampling is sufficient to demonstrate that the acquisition, and performance, of attitudes and behaviors can be a *beneath-conscious* process. Allport (1954) remarked that the process of acquiring prejudicial attitudes seemed to be "infinitely subtle" (p. 293). Pillard (1982) commented as follows on a study by Hastings and Kunnes (1967), in which pharmacists consistently charged Black, poorly-dressed medical students significantly more for an identical prescription than they did White, well-dressed medical students: "It is likely that the pharmacists were not aware that they were systematically charging more to Blacks. . . . Prejudice need not consist of conscious feelings" (p. 101). Pillard commented further that the most corrosive aspect of institutionalized prejudice is simply that it is "built into our culture and, therefore, need never be consciously experienced" (p. 101).

Riddle and Sang (1978) identified examples of subtle antigay or heterosexist bias shown by counselors, including suspicions of pathology (simply posting the question of causation of the client's homosexuality implies pathology); emphasis by the counselor on the client's positive heterosexual, and negative homosexual, relationships; and greater exploration of the client's heterosexual rather than homosexual relationships, thereby indicating the greater importance of the former in contrast to the latter (for further discussion of this issue see also Tripp, 1975, and Woodman & Lenna, 1982).

Garfinkle and Morin (1978) investigated psychotherapists' attitudes toward homosexual clients, assuming that value-free psychotherapy does not exist and that psychotherapists are equipped with "built in maps of inference" (p. 109), based on cultural norms that the use to judge homosexual clients. Psychotherapists were presented with identical, hypothetical case histories, except that in one case, the individual was designated as homosexual, whereas in the other, the client was heterosexual. The homosexual client was perceived as significantly less psychologically healthy than was the heterosexual one, and different treatment goals were identified for each. The authors concluded that the personal values of the psychotherapists were the source of the decreased psychological health of the homosexual client.

CONCLUSIONS AND RECOMMENDATIONS

Psychotherapists, as sentient and interactive members of the society in which they live, are exposed to the same sociocultural influences as are any other persons; thus, psychotherapists are products of the society in which they live and are also contributors to the processes of the same society of which they are the product. I share the beliefs of Davison (1982), who asserted that counselors can never make politically and ethically neutral decisions, and London (1964), who stated:

> Moral considerations may dictate, in large part, how the therapist . . . operates in the therapeutic situation. . . . There cannot be any reasonable question but that psychotherapists of all kinds wish to control behavior in some respects; it is obvious that they do, and only incredible stupidity, innocence, or malice would make them say otherwise. (pp. 5, 157)

Because of the emergence in this country in the past decade of a conservative sociopolitical ideology, a renaissance of fundamental religiosity, and AIDS, the *zeitgeist* has grown increasingly antigay. Such influences have an impact, either consciously or imperceptibly, through such processes as instruction, socialization, imitation, and identification, on the consciousnesses of the American people, including those of counselors.

In a real sense, counselor attitudes toward homosexuality that are *self-consciously* suspicious, intolerant, or even hostile, are less potentially damaging to gay clients than are equally negative attitudes that remain unexperienced by the counselor. In the former case, the psychotherapist can recognize the potential destruction that could eventually occur for the client, thereby allowing for the option of a referral to a more accepting colleague.

When the psychotherapist is unaware of his or her negative biases, however, dissatisfaction or actual psychological harm may be the result for the involved client. Counselors need to *deliberately* reassess their *current* attitudes toward homosexuality, because the attitudes of many toward the issue of gay self-determination may have significantly changed as a function of the antigay climate that has evolved in this country in the past decade. It is through the awareness of the existence of antigay biases that the harmful effects of victim blaming may be aborted, by virtue of an appropriate referral, before such effects may exert an unfair and antitherapeutic influence.

Although certain writers in the field of gay psychotherapy have asserted that awareness, and an explicit revelation, of a counselors's antigay biases is essentially sufficient to practice psychotherapy with a gay client (e.g., Thompson & Fishburn, 1977), I believe such a response to be naive and partial, however, genuinely well-intentioned.

Simple awareness of a bias does not render the bias innocuous; awareness is necessary, but not sufficient. The negative biases of the counselor will be communicated to the client, and at once and proportionately, the client will reciprocate by sensing this negativity. The results of such exchanges, however tacit, are nonetheless destructive.

REFERENCES

Allport, G. W. (1954). *The nature of prejudice.* Reading, MA: Addison-Wesley.

Andersen, K. (1984, September 10). For God and country. *Time,* pp. 8–10.

Anderson, C. L. (1982). The effects of a workshop on attitudes of female nursing students toward male homosexuality. *Journal of Homosexuality, 7,* 57–69.

Barr, R. F., & Catts, S. V. (1974). Psychiatric opinion and homosexuality: A short report. *Journal of Homosexuality, 1,* 213–215.

Bayer, R. (1981). *Homosexuality and American psychiatry.* New York: Basic Books.

Beane, J. (1981). "I'd rather be dead than gay": Counseling gay men who are coming out. *Personnel and Guidance Journal, 60,* 222–226.

Bell, A. P., & Weinberg, M. S. (1978). *Homosexuality: A study in diversity among men and women.* New York: Simon & Schuster.

Bem, D. J., & McConnell, H. K. (1970). Testing the self-perception explanation of dissonance phenomena: On the salience of premanipulation attitudes. *Journal of Personality and Social Psychology, 14,* 23–31.

Brudnoy, D. (1976). Homosexuality in America: At 200 years. *Homosexual Counseling Journal, 3,* 10–22.

Bullough, V. L., & Bullough, B. (1977). *Sin, sickness, and sanity: A history of sexual attitudes.* New York: Garland.

Bullough, V. L. (1979). *Homosexuality: A history.* New York: New American Library.

Carey, J. (1984, September 17). Religion and politics: Furor keeps building. *U.S. News & World Report,* pp. 29–30.

Casas, J. M., Brady, S., & Ponterotto, J. G. (1983). Sexual preference biases in counseling: An information processing approach. *Journal of Counseling Psychology, 30,* 139–145.

A Christian country? (1984, September 21). *National Review,* pp. 18–19.

Church, G. J. (1984, November 19). "You ain't seen nothin' yet?" *Time,* pp. 38–41.

Church, G. J. (1986, July 14). Knocking on the bedroom door. *Time,* pp. 23–24.

Churchill, W. (1967). *Homosexual behavior among males: A cross-cultural and cross-species investigation.* New York: Hawthorn.

Clark, G. (1985, August 12). In the middle of a war. *Time,* p. 46.

Clark, M. F. (1979). Attitudes, information, and behavior of counselors toward homosexual clients. *Dissertation Abstracts International, 40,* 5729A.

Davison, G. C., & Wilson, G. T. (1973). Attitudes of behavior therapists toward homosexuality. *Behavior Therapy, 4,* 686–696.

Davison, G. C. (1982). Politics, ethics, and therapy for homosexuality. In W. Paul, J. D. Weinrich, J. C. Gonsiorek, & M. E. Hotvedt (Eds.), *Homosexuality: Social, psychological, and biological issues* (pp. 89–98). Beverly Hills, CA: Sage.

Douglas, C. J., Kalman, C. M., & Kalman, T. P. (1985). Homophobia among physicians and nurses: An empirical study. *Hospital and Community Psychiatry, 36,* 1309–1311.

Escoffier, J. (1975). Stigmas, work environment, and economic discrimination against homosexuals. *Homosexual Counseling Journal, 2,* 8–17.

Fairlie, H. (1981, January 31). Who speaks for values? *The New Republic,* pp. 17–19.

Fischer, T. R. (1982). A study of educators' attitudes toward homosexuality. *Dissertation Abstracts International, 43,* 3294A.

Fisher, P. (1972). *The gay mystique.* New York: Stein & Day.

Fort, J., Steiner, C. M., & Conrad, R. (1971). Attitudes of mental health professionals toward homosexuality and its treatment. *Psychological Reports, 29,* 347–350.

Gallup, G. (1975a). *The Gallup opinion index* (Report No. 114). Princeton, NJ: The American Institute of Public Opinion.

Gallup, G. (1975b). *The Gallup opinion index* (Report No. 116). Princeton, NJ: The American Institute of Public Opinion.

Gallup, G. (1976). *The Gallup opinion index* (Report No. 130). Princeton, NJ: The American Institute of Public Opinion.

Gallup, G. (1977a). *The Gallup opinion index* (Report No. 145). Princeton, NJ: The American Institute of Public Opinion.

Gallup, G. (1977b). *The Gallup opinion index* (Report No. 147). Princeton, NJ: The American Institute of Public Opinion.

Gallup, G. (1979). *The Gallup opinion index* (Report No. 170). Princeton, NJ: The American Institute of Public Opinion.

Gallup, G. (1980). *The Gallup opinion index* (Report No. 177). Princeton, NJ: The American Institute of Public Opinion.

Gallup, G. (1982a). *The Gallup opinion index* (Report No. 197). Princeton, NJ: The American Institute of Public Opinion.

Gallup, G. (1982b). *The Gallup opinion index* (Report No. 198). Princeton, NJ: The American Institute of Public Opinion.

Gallup, G. (1982c). *The Gallup opinion index* (Report Nos. 201–202). Princeton, NJ: The American Institute of Public Opinion.

Gallup, G. (1982d). *The Gallup opinion index* (Report No. 204). Princeton, NJ: The American Institute of Public Opinion.

Gallup, G. (1982e). *The Gallup opinion index* (Report No. 205). Princeton, NJ: The American Institute of Public Opinion.

Gallup, G. (1983a). *The Gallup opinion index* (Report No. 215). Princeton, NJ: The American Institute of Public Opinion.

Gallup, G. (1983b). *The Gallup opinion index* (Report No. 216). Princeton, NJ: The American Institute of Public Opinion.

Gallup, G. (1984a). *The Gallup opinion index* (Report No. 222). Princeton, NJ: The American Institute of Public Opinion.

Gallup, G. (1984b). *The Gallup opinion index* (Report No. 230). Princeton, NJ: The American Institute of Public Opinion.

Gallup, G. (1985). *The Gallup opinion index* (Report No. 236). Princeton, NJ: The American Institute of Public Opinion.

Gallup, G. (1986). *The Gallup opinion index* (Report No. 249). Princeton, NJ: The American Institute of Public Opinion.

Garfinkle, E. M., & Morin, S. F. (1978). Psychologists' attitudes toward homosexual psychotherapy clients. *Journal of Social Issues, 34,* 101–112.

Gartrell, N., Kraemer, H., & Brodie, H. K. H. (1974). Psychiatrists' attitudes toward female homosexuality. *The Journal of Nervous and Mental Disease, 150,* 141–144.

Goethals, G. R., & Reckman, R. F. (1973). The perception of consistency in attitudes. *Journal of Experimental Social Psychology, 9,* 491–501.

Gold, R. (1973). A symposium: Should homosexuality be in the APA nomenclature. *The American Journal of Psychiatry, 130,* 1207–1216.

Greenspoon, J. (1955). The reinforcing effect of two spoken sounds on the frequency of two responses. *The American Journal of Psychology, 68,* 409–416.

Harris, L. (1986). *The Harris Survey* (Report No. 17). New York: Louis Harris.

Hart, M., Roback, H. H., Tittler, T., Weitz, L., Walston, B., & McKee, E. (1978). Psychological adjustment of nonpatient homosexuals: Critical review of the research literature. *Journal of Clinical Psychiatry, 39,* 604–608.

Hastings, G. E. & Kunnes, R. (1967). Predicting prescription prices. *New England Journal of Medicine, 277,* 625–628.

Hyman, R. A. (1980). A comparison of methods for changing homophobic attitudes of mental health professionals: The effects of cognitive vs. affective and homosexuality vs. homophobia approaches. *Dissertation Abstracts International, 40,* 6201A.

Ivey, R. D. (1972). Consultation with a male homosexual. *Personnel and Guidance Journal, 50,* 749–754.

Kameny, F. E. (1972). Gay liberation and psychiatry. In J. A. McCaffrey (Ed.), *The homosexual dialectic* (pp. 182–194). Englewood Cliffs, NJ: Prentice-Hall.

Killinger, R. R. (1971). The counselor and gay liberation. *Personnel and Guidance Journal, 49,* 715–719.

Kingdon, M. A. (1979). Lesbians. *The Counseling Psychologist, 8*(1), 44–45.

Kinsey, A. C., Pomeroy, W. B., & Martin, C. E. (1948). *Sexual behavior in the human male.* New York: Saunders.

Kinsey, A. C., Pomeroy, W. B., Martin, C. E., & Gebhard, P. H. (1953). *Sexual behavior in the human female.* Philadelphia: Saunders.

Kopkind, A. (1984, November 3). The age of Reaganism. *The Nation,* p. 433.

Latane, B., & Darley, J. M. (1970). *The unresponsive bystander: Why doesn't he help?* New York: Appleton-Century-Crofts.

Leerhsen, C. (1985, September 23). "Hard times ahead": Gays brace for wave of homophobia. *Newsweek,* p. 24.

Leo, J. (1986, November 24). Sex and schools. *Time,* pp. 54–63.

Levine, M. P. (1980). Employment discrimination against gay men. In J. Harry & M. S. Das (Eds.), *Homosexuality in international perspective* (pp. 18–30). New York: Advent.

Levitt, E. E., & Klassen, A. D. (1974). Public attitudes toward homosexuality: Part of the 1970 national survey by the Institute for Sex Research. *Journal of Homosexuality, 1,* 28–43.

London, P. (1964). *The modes and morals of psychotherapy.* New York: Holt, Rinehart, and Winston.

McCann-Winter, E. J. S. (1983). Clergy education about homosexuality: An outcomes analysis of knowledge, attitudes, and counseling behavior (Doctoral dissertation, University of Pennsylvania, 1983). *Dissertation Abstracts International, 44,* 675A.

MacDonald, A. P. (1976). Homophobia: Its roots and meanings. *Homosexual Counseling Journal, 3,* 23–33.

McIntosh, M. (1968). The homosexual role. *Social Problems, 16,* 182–192.

Morris, P. A. (1973). Doctors' attitudes to homosexuality, *British Journal of Psychiatry, 122,* 435–436.

Morrow, L. (1985, September 23). The start of a plague mentality, *Time,* p. 92.

Moses, A. E., & Hawkins, Jr., R. D. (1982). *Counseling lesbian women and gay men.* St. Louis: Mosby.

National Opinion Research Center (1985). *General social surveys, 1972–1985: Cumulative codebook.* Chicago: University of Chicago.

Nelson, J. B. (1982). Religious and moral issues in working with homosexual clients. In J. C. Gonsiorek (Ed.), *Homosexuality and psychotherapy* (pp. 163–175). New York: Haworth.

Nisbett, R. E., & Wilson, T. D. (1977). Telling more than we can know: Verbal reports on mental processes. *Psychological Review 84,* 231–259.

Norton, J. L. (1982). Integrating gay issues into counselor education. *Counselor Education and Supervision, 21,* 208–212.

Nuehring, E. M., Fein, S. B., & Tyler, M. (1974). The gay college student: Perspectives for mental health professionals. *The Counseling Psychologist, 4*(4), 64–72.

Ostling, R. N. (1985, September 2). Jerry Falwell's crusade. *Time,* pp. 48–57.

Pauly, I. B., & Goldstein, S. B. (1970). Physicians' attitudes in treating male homosexuals. *Medical Aspects of Human Sexuality, 4*(12), 26–45.

Pillard, R. C. (1982). Psychotherapeutic treatment for the invisible minority. In W. Paul, J. D. Weinrich, J. C. Gonsiorek, & M. E. Hotvedt (Eds.), *Homosexuality: Social, psychological, and biological issues* (pp. 99–113). Beverly Hills, CA: Sage.

Poll on socio-medical issues. (1969). *Modern Medicine, 37*(22), 18–25.

Protestants: Away from activism and back to the basics. (1977, April 11). *U.S. News & World Report,* pp. 58–62.

Riddle, D. I., & Snag, B. (1978). Psychotherapy with lesbians. *Journal of Social Issues, 34,* 84–100.

Roman, M., Charles, E., & Karasu, T. B. (1978). The value systems of psychotherapists and changing mores. *Psychotherapy: Theory, Research, & Practice, 15,* 409–415.

Rosenblatt, R. (1984, November 19). Reagan country. *Time,* pp. 36–37.

Saghir, M. T., Robins, E., Walbran, B., & Gentry, K. A. (1970a). Psychiatric disorders and disability in the male homosexual. *American Journal of Psychiatry, 126,* 1079–1086.

Saghir, M. T., Robins, E., Walbran, B., & Gentry, K. A. (1970b). Psychiatric disorders and disability in the female homosexual. *American Journal of Psychiatry, 127,* 147–154.

Stacks, J. F. (198, June 1). It's rightward on. *Time,* pp. 12–13.

Thomas, E. (1985, September 23). The new untouchables. *Time,* pp. 24–26.

Thompson, G. J., & Fishburn, W. R. (1977). Attitudes toward homosexuality among graduate counseling students. *Counselor Education and Supervision, 17,* 121–130.

A time for renewal of U.S. churches. (1977, April 11). *U.S. News World Report,* pp. 54–57.

Tripp, C. A. (1975). *The homosexual matrix.* New York: McGraw-Hill.

Wallis, C. (1985, August 12). AIDS: A growing threat. *Time,* pp. 40–47.

Weinberg, G. (1972). *Society and the healthy homosexual.* New York: St. Martins.

West, D. J. (1977). *Homosexuality re-examined.* Minneapolis: University of Minnesota.

White, T. H. (1984, November 19). The shaping of the presidency 1984. *Time,* pp. 70–83.

Woodman, N. J., & Lenna, H. R. (1982). *Counseling with gay men and women.* San Francisco: Jossey-Bass.

ARVIC as a Child of Ten

There is a stillness in the recording of birthdays
  a silence
  almost a reverence
as a moment comes quickly
  and like the fleeting breath of a child
  blowing out the candles on a cake
  disappears into the flow of time.
Yet in the quietness there is hope
  an expectation beyond the mundane
  a faith that transcends the wish of the moment.

ARVIC, we have known you since birth.
  Amazed and proud, like surrogate parents,
  We have watched you grow.
  You have brought us joy
  in the midst of struggles,
  and added the warmth of a childlike wonder
  to the coolness of our lives.
Many of us bask shyly in the knowledge
  that we helped give you life;
Others carry pictures in their minds
  of your initial toddler steps
  and like proud relatives
  gladly show off the memories in colorful stories
  framed in the events of time.
All of us in some way now claim you as our own!
When we speak of you, it is with awe,
  for we know that as a child reflects its heritage
  so we find at least a part of ourselves in you.

Yet our identity goes beyond kinship or possession.
We realize that relationships and network dreams
  have a life of their own
  that is always evolving.
If we tried to capture your mystery
  it would be as futile as trying to calm the wind
  that keeps candles from burning
  after a young child has blow on them.
So, we celebrate your presence
  Your ecumenical spirit that unites us
  in our quest for truth,

We look forward to your growth
  the adolescent years, young adulthood,
  middle age, and beyond.
As you increase, so do we
  in spirit, in hope,
  and in kindness,
Until amid the wrinkles that come with the passing of days
  as we reflect on our own special memories
We may say to ourselves with a smile
"ARVIC I knew and loved you as a child."

                                        Samuel T. Gladding

DATE DUE

HIGHSMITH 45-220